Rites and Rituals

Comparing Times and Cultures

Play selection and
resource material by

Steve Lewis

Series Consultant

Cecily O'Neill

Published by Collins Educational, an imprint of HarperCollins*Publishers* Ltd, 77–85 Fulham Palace Road, London W6 8JB

www.**Collins**Education.com
On-line support for schools and colleges

First published 2004

ISBN 000 713144 5

British Library Cataloguing in Publication Data

A catalogue record for this book is available from the British Library.

Commissioned by Isabelle Zahar, edited by Gaynor Spry and Mark Dudgeon, picture research by Mark Dudgeon

Design by Jordan Publishing Design, cover design by Jordan Publishing Design, cover photograph of *The Importance of Being Earnest* © Donald Cooper/Photostage

Special thanks to: Andy, Annie and Chris, Dona and Mike, Graham and Tracie, Jacqui, Jill, Julia, Laurie, Lorna, Mandy and John, Nan, Stuart and Corinne and Richard, for your love, friendship and support.

Acknowledgements

The following permissions to reproduce material are gratefully acknowledged:

Photographs: © 2003 Picture History LLC, p7; courtesy of The Royal National Theatre and © Nobby Clark, p24; *The Picnic*, by James Tissot © Bridgeman Art Library, p53; *The Proposal*, by Alfred W. Elmore © Christies Images Ltd, p58; © Donald Cooper/Photostage, p81; © AA World Travel Library, p111.

Text Extracts: *A Respectable Wedding* from *Brecht Plays 1*, ed. Willett/Manheim, translated by Jean Benedetti, Methuen Publishing Ltd; *Two Marias* by Bryony Lavery, Methuen Publishing Ltd; *Blood Wedding* by Federico Garcia Lorca, Methuen Publishing Ltd; *The Love Letters of Ragie Patel* by Lee Hall, © Lee Hall 1997, first broadcast by the BBC; *Four Weddings and a Funeral* 1994 by kind permission of Richard Curtis c/o The Peters Fraser and Dunlop Group; *Spoonface Steinberg and Other Plays* by Lee Hall reproduced with the permission of BBC Worldwide Limited, © Lee Hall 1997.

Every effort has been made to trace copyright holders, but in some cases this has proved impossible. The publishers would be happy to hear from any copyright holder that has not been acknowledged.

Production by Katie Morris, printed and bound by Imago.

You might also like to visit
www.harpercollins.co.uk
The book lover's website

Contents

KEY		
71–74 71–74	cross-reference between playscript and teaching resources.	

Introduction

The four play extracts in this collection provide an illustration of the ways in which playwrights in the 19th and 20th centuries have dealt with the rites and rituals surrounding love and death.

- *The Shaughraun* is set around an Irish wake. Conn, the shaughraun or scoundrel of the title, comes to life during his own funeral to confront his "killers". The events are worked out in a truly Victorian melodramatic fashion.

- *The Importance of Being Earnest* shows Wilde's witty version of a marriage proposal scene between Ernest (or should that be Jack?) and the independent-minded Gwendolen, whose mother, Lady Bracknell, has strong views about whom her daughter should marry.

- *A Respectable Wedding* takes place at a wedding reception and illustrates the underlying tensions between the families of the bride and bridegroom who have been brought together for this ritual. The bridegroom has made all his own furniture and the fact that most of it is in danger of collapse during the play, suggests that the marriage is starting on rather shaky ground.

- *Two Marias* explores the bizarre story of a mother who believes that her daughter had survived a car accident. It slowly emerges that it was, in fact, her daughter that was killed and that the girl in the hospital belongs to another family. The play is a ritual working-out of the grief surrounding the loss of a child by a mother.

This selection of plays and resources are suitable for study, exploration and/or performance within the GCSE Drama specifications offered by AQA, Edexcel, OCR and WJEC. The extracts make complete short plays in their own right and can be used effectively for the performance component for any GCSE Drama course. Each extract lasts between fifteen and twenty minutes.

Extract 1 (from *The Shaughraun*) requires a cast of seven males (or six males with one actor playing both Father Dolan and Donovan) and four females (or three females with one actor playing both Claire and Nancy) with an additional number of extras to play peasants.

Extract 2 (from *The Importance of Being Earnest*) requires a cast of two females and one male.

Extract 3 (from *A Respectable Wedding*) requires a cast of four females and five males.

Extract 4 (from *Two Marias*) requires a cast of four females.

AQA DRAMA COURSEWORK COVERAGE CHART

Candidates taking the AQA GCSE Drama course must offer two different options for coursework: one from the list of Scripted Work options and one from the list of Unscripted Work options. At least one of these must be a performance option. Where a technical and design skill option is undertaken, it must contribute to a group performance. Each option is divided into three parts, with each part testing a different Assessment Objective (AO).

AO1 Final presentation (either performance or demonstration/ artefacts), in which candidates are assessed on their ability to *"demonstrate ability in and knowledge and understanding of the practical skills in drama necessary for the realisation of a presentation to an audience, working constructively with others."*

AO2 Response to plays and other types of drama, in which candidates are assessed on their ability to *"respond with knowledge and understanding to plays and other types of drama from a performance perspective and to explore relationships and comparisons between texts and dramatic styles of different periods and of different cultures in order to show an awareness of their social context and genre."*

AO3 Work in progress, in which candidates are assessed on their ability to *"analyse and evaluate the effectiveness of their own and others' work with sensitivity as they develop and present their work in an appropriate format for communication."*

AQA coursework option	1. The Shaughraun	2. The Importance of Being Earnest	3. A Respectable Wedding	4. Two Marias	Comparing the four extracts
Option 1: Devised thematic work		2f; 2g	3j; 3m	4j; 4l	5c; 5f
Option 2: Acting	1e; 1f; 1g; 1h	2c; 2d; 2e; 2f	3e; 3f; 3g; 3h; 3i; 3j; 3k	4f; 4g; 4h; 4i, 4j; 4k	
Option 6: Set	1a	2a	3b	4a; 4b	
Option 7: Costume	1c	2b	3c	4c p.94	
Option 8: Make-up	*	*	*	*	
Option 9: Properties	1b		3a	4b	
Option 10: Masks					
Option 11: Puppets					
Option 12: Lighting	1d	p.45	p.70	4d	
Option 13: Sound	p.24	p.45	p.71		
Option 14: Stage management	†	†	†	†	

* Make-up can be used in all of the plays
† All these plays can be used as stage management texts

EDEXCEL DRAMA COURSEWORK COVERAGE CHART

The chart below highlights which activities provide opportunities or guidance for work on the Edexcel Paper 1, Units 1 and 2: Drama Exploration. In the workshops for this paper, to be based around at least two different types of drama texts, candidates are required to use a) at least four of the explorative strategies, b) at least two of the drama skill areas, and c) to select and use appropriately the elements of drama in their practical and written responses to the stimulus material.

Edexcel c/w strategies, skills and elements of drama	1. The Shaughraun	2. The Importance of Being Earnest	3. A Respectable Wedding	4. Two Marias	Comparing the four extracts
(a) Explorative Strategies					
Still image	1e	2g		4f	5e
Thought-tracking	1f		3k	4i	
Narrating		2f		4g	
Hot-seating		2d	3i		
Role-play	1j	2e	3j	4j; 4l	5c
Cross-cutting					
Forum-theatre	1g				
Marking the moment					

Edexcel c/w strategies, skills and elements of drama	1. The Shaughraun	2. The Importance of Being Earnest	3. A Respectable Wedding	4. Two Marias	Comparing the four extracts
(b) The Drama Medium					
Use of costume, masks, make-up	1c	2b	3c	4c p.94	5c and 5f apply to all areas
Sound/music	p.24	p.45	p.71		
Lighting	1d	p.45	p.70	4d	
Space/levels	1a	2a	3a	4a	
Set and props	1a; 1b	2a	3a; 3b	4a; 4b	
Movement, mime, gesture	1g	2g	3e; 3f	4j; 4l	
Voice	1k	2c; 2f; 2g	3e; 3f	4j; 4l	
Spoken language	1k	2c; 2f; 2g	3e; 3f	4g; 4j; 4l	
(c) The Elements of Drama					
Action/plot/content	See section headed "Summary of the plot" to each play				
Forms	See section headed "Genre and subject matter" to each play				
Climax/anticlimax			3e; 3f	4f	5c and 5f apply to all areas
Rhythm/pace/tempo			3e; 3f	4f	
Contrasts			3e; 3f	4l	
Characterisation	1h; 1i; 1j	2d; 2e; 2f	3g; 3h; 3i; 3j; 3k	4f; 4g; 4h; 4i; 4j 4k	
Conventions	1e	2f		4f; 4g; 4l	
Symbols				4f	

ENGLISH FRAMEWORK OBJECTIVES CHART

Edexcel Framework Objective	1. The Shaughraun	2. The Importance of Being Earnest	3. A Respectable Wedding	4. Two Marias	Comparing the four extracts
Comment on the authorial perspectives offered in texts on individuals, community and society in texts from different cultures (R6)	This objective can be covered through the study of any of the plays in this collection.				
Compare the presentation of ideas, values or emotions in related or contrasting texts (R7)	1l	2h	3l; 3m	4e; 4l; 4m	5a; 5b; 5d; 5e
Analyze the language, form and dramatic impact of scenes and plays by published dramatists (R14)	This objective can be covered through the study of any of the plays in this collection.				
Analyze ways in which different cultural contexts and traditions have influenced language and style (R16)	This objective can be covered through the study of any of the plays in this collection.				
Recognize, evaluate and extend the skills and techniques they have developed through drama (S&L11)	1e; 1f; 1g	2d; 2e	3i; 3j; 3k	4f; 4h; 4i; 4j; 4k 4l	
Use a range of drama techniques, including work in role, to explore issues, ideas and meanings (S&L12)	1j	2d; 2e; 2f; 2g	3d; 3i; 3j; 3k	4f; 4h; 4i; 4j; 4k 4l	5c
Develop and compare different interpretations of scenes or plays by Shakespeare or other dramatists (S&L13)	This objective can be covered through the study of any of the plays in this collection.				
Convey action, character, atmosphere and tension when scripting and performing plays (S&L14)		2e; 2f; 2g	3m	4g; 4j; 4l	5c; 5f
Write critical evaluations of performances they have seen or in which they have participated, identifying the contributions of the writer, director and actors (S&L15)	This objective can be covered if any of the plays are seen in live performance or pupils compare their own performances of the extracts.				

The Shaughraun

Dion Boucicault

DION BOUCICAULT

Dion Boucicault's life was as adventurous and colourful as that of the characters in the 200 or so plays that he wrote, adapted or translated. He wrote the part of Conn, the Shaughraun (pronounced *shoch-rawn*) with himself in mind and played the part to great acclaim. Born in Dublin in 1820 and christened Dionysus Lardner Boursiquot, he later became known as Dion Boucicault (pronounced *Boo-see-ko*) and was both famous and infamous for his performances on and off the stage. He was married three times, the third time at the age of 65 to a 21-year-old actress, claiming that he had never really married his second wife and thereby dispossessing his children. The plays that he produced were lavish spectacles and he was a master at creating special effects. Despite his immense popularity as a playwright and showman during his lifetime, by the time of his death in 1890, his work had largely gone out of fashion in the British theatre, but Boucicault's three comic melodramas set in Ireland – *The Colleen Bawn* (1860), *Arrah-na Pogue* (1864) and *The Shaughraun* (1874) – remain popular in the Irish repertoire to this day.

SUMMARY OF THE PLOT

The Shaughraun is a plot-driven play with complicated twists and turns brought about by the deeds and misdeeds of the characters. Set in British-ruled Ireland in the 1870s, the play follows the fates of Conn O'Kelly – the Shaughraun, or boisterous rogue – of the title, his friends Robert Ffolliott and his sister Claire Ffolliott, and the treacherous Corry

Kinchela. Contriving to seize the Ffolliott estate for himself, Kinchela engineers Robert's arrest and imprisonment in Australia for his involvement with the Fenian Brotherhood – a political organization seeking Irish independence. Helped to escape and return to Ireland by Conn, Robert has to avoid arrest by Captain Molineux of the British Army, who finds his own loyalty tested as he falls in love with Robert's sister, Claire.

Kinchela again plots for Robert's imprisonment by seeming to help him escape, only to have him imprisoned a second time with the help of his henchman, Harvey Duff, and the local constabulary.

Conn once more helps his friend to escape prison and evade their pursuers to make his way towards the coast and an awaiting boat. Disguised as Robert, Conn draws Kinchela's pursuing men to himself. When he is shot it is assumed that Robert has been killed. Too late, Kinchela realizes that the shots provide the signal for the rescue boat and they see Robert making his escape below. It is not Robert whom they have shot, but Conn, the Shaughraun.

THE SCENE IN CONTEXT

The extract is from the start of Act Three of the play in which we find that Conn is not dead at all but uses his funeral to trap two of Kinchela's men. The two men, Reilly and Sullivan, are left with no option but to lead Conn and Captain Molineaux to the place where his beloved Moya and Robert's fiancée, Arte, have been kidnapped by Kinchela.

The remaining scenes of the play deal with the hunt for the treacherous Kinchela who is preparing to escape to sea, taking Arte and Moya with him, and his eventual arrest by Captain Molineux. Molineux finds a royal pardon for Robert in Kinchela's pocket and Robert is at last a free man and reunited with his beloved Arte. Molineux proposes marriage to Claire and she accepts. Father Dolan needs reassurance from his daughter Moya that she will tame Conn's wild ways before giving his consent to their marriage. Conn asks the audience to back him in his cause and the play ends with the prospect of a triple wedding.

The Shaughraun

By

Dion Boucicault – Ireland

CAST LIST

FATHER DOLAN the parish priest of Suil-a-beg, tutor and guardian to Robert

CLAIRE FFOLLIOTT a Sligo lady

MRS O'KELLY Conn's mother

CAPTAIN MOLINEUX a young English officer commanding a detachment at Ballyragget

CONN the shaughraun, the soul of every fair, the life of every funeral, the first fiddle at all weddings and patterns

ROBERT FFOLLIOTT a young Irish gentleman, under sentence as a Fenian

NANCY MALONE a keener

BIDDY MADIGAN a keener

REILLY a peasant

SULLIVAN a peasant

DONOVAN a peasant

COMPANY OF PEASANTS (the actors playing **Father Dolan**, **Claire** and **Robert** in Scene One can double up as **peasants** in Scene Two)

Scene One

Mrs O'Kelly's Cottage; bar of window undone. Music.

*Enter **Molineux**, **Father Dolan** and **Claire**.*

MOLINEUX I've been thinking.

CLAIRE Thinking! what's the good of thinking? My cousin Arte has been stolen – where is she? The country is full of police and soldiers, and yet two girls have been carried off under your noses – perhaps murdered, for all you know or care – and there you stand like a goose, thinking!

MOLINEUX Pray don't be so impetuous. You Irish –

CLAIRE I won't be called 'You Irish'.

MOLINEUX I beg your pardon; you do make me so nervous.

CLAIRE Oh, do I? My impetuosity didn't make you nervous last night, did it? No matter! go on – a penny for your thoughts.

MOLINEUX If Miss O'Neal and Moya were present in the ruins when Conn was shot, they must have been witnesses of the deed. Since then they have disappeared. It struck me that those who killed the boy must have some reason for removing all evidence of the transaction.

FATHER DOLAN He is right.

CLAIRE Well?

MOLINEUX I questioned the constabulary, and find they had no hand in it. The deed was done by a posse of fellows assembled to assist in the pursuit by a police agent named Harvey Duff.

FATHER DOLAN AND CLAIRE Harvey Duff!

MOLINEUX You know him?

CLAIRE He has thought it out while we have been blundering. Blinded by our tears, we could not see; deafened by our complaints, we could not hear. *(seizes both his hands)* Forgive me!

MOLINEUX There she goes again! I've done nothing to deserve all this.

CLAIRE Nothing! You have unearthed the fox, you have drawn the badger; now the rogue is in sight our course is clear.

MOLINEUX It is? I confess I don't see it!

FATHER DOLAN These two girls were the only witnesses of the deed!

CLAIRE And that is why they have been carried off.

FATHER DOLAN No one else was present to prove how Conn was killed.

CONN *(looking out of the window)* Yes; I was there!

ALL Conn alive!

CONN Whisht! No; I'm dead!

FATHER DOLAN Why, you provoking vagabond – is this the way you play upon our feelings? Are you hurt?

CONN I've a crack over the lug, an' a scratch across the small o' me back. Sure, miss, if I hadn't dhrawed them to shoot, you'd have never had the signal.

MOLINEUX Brave fellow! how did you escape?

CONN I'll tell you, sir; but – whoo! gorra! – dead men tell no tales, an' here I am takin' away the character of the corporation. When the masther got out of gaol, there was Kinchela an' his gang waitin' outside to murdher us. We ga' them the slip; and while the masther got off, I led them away afther me to St Bridget's. Then, after I got them two shots out o' them, I rouled down an' lay as quiet as a sack of pitaties.

30

CLAIRE Arte and Moya were in the ruins?

CONN They were standing by and thrying to screech blue murdher. 'Stop their mouths', said a voice that I knew was Kinchela's. Sullivan and Reilly whipt them up and put them on a car that was waitin' outside. After that, sorra a thing I remember till I found myself laid out on a shutter, wid candles all round me, an' whiskey bottles, an' cakes, an' sugar, an' lemon, an' tobacco, an' bacon, an' snuff, an' the devil in all! I thought I was in Heaven.

FATHER DOLAN And that's his idea of Heaven! And you let your poor ould mother believe you dead – you did not relieve her sorrow?

CONN Would you have me spile a wake afther invitin' all the neighbours?

MOLINEUX Will you allow me on this occasion to say, 'You Irish – '

CLAIRE Yes, and you need not say any more.

CONN Then I remembered the polis would be wanting me for the share I had in helping the masther to break gaol. Ah, sir, don't let on to the mother – she'd never hould her whisht; an' I want to be dead, if yez plaze, to folly up the blackguards that have hoult of Moya and Miss O'Neal.

MOLINEUX Do you know the place where these ruffians resort?

CONN I'm concaited I do.

FATHER DOLAN I'll answer for him; he knows every disreputable den in the country.

CONN What would you do now if I didn't?

CLAIRE Here comes your mother with the mourners.

CONN Hoo! she'll find some of the whiskey gone. *(disappears)*

CLAIRE Now what's to be done?

MOLINEUX I will proceed at once to Ballyragget House, and see Mr Kinchela. I shall take a guard and arrest him for aiding your brother to escape, that he might murder him safely during his flight.

CLAIRE Who can prove it?

*Enter **Robert**.*

ROBERT I can!

CLAIRE Robert!

They embrace.

FATHER DOLAN Good gracious, what brings you back?

ROBERT The news I heard on board the schooner. A pardon has been granted to the Fenian prisoners.

CLAIRE A pardon!

MOLINEUX I congratulate you, sir. *(shakes hands with **Robert**)* Oh, by Jove! Excuse my swearing, but a light breaks in upon me – Kinchela knew of this pardon. I'll go to Ballyragget House at once.

ROBERT I have just come from there. I went to tax him with his villainy. He has fled.

MOLINEUX I thought there was no fight in him.

CLAIRE But Arte is in his power.

ROBERT Arte in his power! What do you mean?

CLAIRE He loves her – he has carried her off.

ROBERT My wife and her fortune! Ha! he played for a high game.

MOLINEUX And on finding he could not win, he stole half the stakes.

FATHER DOLAN This man is in league with a desperate crew, half ruffians, half smugglers. Their dens, known only to themselves, are in the bogs and caves of the sea-shore.

ROBERT I'll unearth him wherever he is. *(music)* I'll hunt him with every honest lad of the County Sligo in the pack, and kill him like a rat.

MOLINEUX I'll send over to Sligo, and get a warrant to arrest this fellow. I like to have the law on my side. If we are to have a hunt, let us have a licence. Where shall I find you?

FATHER DOLAN At my house.

CLAIRE *(to **Robert**, who offers his arm to her)* No, give your arm to Father Dolan.

FATHER DOLAN Free, and at home! Heaven be praised!

ROBERT Not free till Arte is so. *(exit with **Father Dolan**)*

CLAIRE *(after watching them off, turns and advances rapidly to **Molineux**)* What's your Christian name, or have you English such things amongst you?

MOLINEUX Yes; my Christian name is Harry.

CLAIRE Harry!

Kissing him; she runs off. He assumes a military position and marches off, whistling 'The British Grenadiers'.

VOICES *(outside)* Oh! Ohone! Oh, hould up. Don't give way.

*Enter **Mrs O'Kelly**, **Nancy Malone**, **Biddy Madigan**, **Donovan** and **peasants**.*

MRS O'KELLY You are kindly welcome. The dark cloud is over the house, but –

NANCY We come to share the sorrow that's in it this hour.

BIDDY It will be a fine berryin', Mrs O'Kelly. There will be a grand waste of victuals.

MRS O'KELLY Step inside, ma'am.

*They all enter the cabin. A **woman** enters, and exits into cabin. Then **Reilly**, followed by **Sullivan**. Music. The voices of the **keeners** are heard inside singing an Irish lament. During this, other **peasants** and **girls** enter in couples, and go into cabin. Scene changes.*

Scene Two

21 *Mrs O'Kelly's Cabin. The interior. Door, R., fireplace, R. **Conn** is lying on a shutter, L., supported by an old table, a three-legged stool, and a keg. Table, R., covered with food and drinking cups, plates of snuff, jugs of punch, lighted candles in bottles, etc. Tableau of an Irish Wake. A group of women around **Conn**. **Mrs O'Kelly** seated, L.C. **Nancy Malone** and **Reilly** near her, seated R. **Sullivan**, **Donovan** and **peasantry** (male and female) at table, R. The **women** seated are rocking to and fro during the wail.*

Chorus 'The Oolaghaun.'

Male Voices 'Och, Oolaghaun! och, Oolaghaun!
Make his bed both wide and deep!
Och, Oolaghaun! och, Oolaghaun!
He's only gone to sleep!

Female Voices Why did ye die? oh, why did ye die?
And lave us all alone to cry?

Together Why did ye die? why did ye die?
Laving us to sigh, och hone!
Why did ye die? why did ye die?
Oolaghaun! oh, Oolaghaun!

*During the following rhapsody the music of the wail and the chorus,
subdued, recurs as if to animate the* **keeners**.

Biddy Oh, oh, oho! *(rocking herself)* Oh, oo, Oolaghaun! The widdy
had a son – an only son – wail for the widdy!

All Why did ye die? why did ye die?

Biddy I see her when she was a fair young girl – a fine girl, wid a
child at her breast.

All Laving us to sigh! Och, hone!

Biddy Then I see a proud woman wid a boy by her side. He was as
bould as a bull-calf that runs beside of the cow.

All Why did ye die? why did ye die?

Biddy For the girl grew ould as the child grew big, and the woman
grew wake as the boy grew strong. *(rising and flinging back her
hair)* The boy grew strong, for she fed him wid her heart's blood.
Ah, hoogoola! Where is he now? Cowld in his bed! Why did ye
die? *(sits)*

All Leaving us to sigh! Och, hone!

Biddy None was like him – none could compare, and – good luck
to ye, gi' me a dhrop of somethin' to put the sperret in one, for
the fire's getting low.

Sullivan *hands her his jug of punch.*

Mrs O'Kelly Oh, oh! it's mighty consolin' to hear this Mrs Malone, you are not ating?

Nancy No, ma'am, I'm dhrinkin'. I dhrink now and agin by way of variety. Biddy is not up to herself.

Reilly Oh, wait till she'll rise on the top of a noggin.

Biddy *(after drinking places the jug beside her, and rises on low stool)* He was brave! he was brave! he was openhanded! he had the heart of a lion, and the legs of a fox.

Conn *takes the jug, empties is quietly, and, unobserved by all, replaces it on stool.*

Biddy His voice was softer than the cuckoo of an evening, and sweeter than the blackbird afther a summer shower. Ye colleens, ye will nivir hear the voice of Conn again. *(sits and blows her nose)*

Conn *(aside)* It's a mighty pleasant thing to die like this, once in a way, and hear all the good things said about ye afther you're dead and gone, when they can do you no good.

Biddy His name will be the pride of the O'Kellys for evermore.

Conn *(aside)* I was a big blackguard when I was alive.

Biddy Noble and beautiful!

Conn *(aside)* Ah go on out o' that!

Biddy *(taking up her jug)* Oh, he was sweet and sthrong – who the divil's been at my jug of punch?

Mrs O'Kelly *(sobbing and rising)* Nobody is dhrinking – yez all despise the occasion – if yez lave behind ye liquor enough to swim a fly – oh, hoo! There's a hole in your mug, Mr Donovan; I'd be glad to see it in the bottle – oh, hoo!

Knock without.

Sullivan What's that?

The door is opened.

Enter **Molineux**. *They all rise.*

MOLINEUX I don't come to disturb this – a – melancholy – a – entertainment – I mean – a – this festive solemnity –

MRS O'KELLY *(wiping own chair for him with her apron)* Heaven bless you for coming to admire the last of him. Here he is – ain't he beautiful?

MOLINEUX *(aside)* The vagabond is winking at me. I've a great mind to kick the keg from under him and send him reeling on the floor.

MRS O'KELLY How often have I put him to bed as a child, and sung him to sleep! Now he will be put to bed with a shovel, and oh! the song was nivir sung that will awaken him.

MOLINEUX If any words could put life into him, I came here to speak them. *(music)* Robert Ffolliott has been pardoned and has returned home a free man.

ALL Hurroo! hurroo!

MOLINEUX But his home is desolate, for the girl he loves has been stolen away. The man who robbed him of his liberty first, then his estate, has now stolen his betrothed.

ALL Who is it?

MOLINEUX Mr Corry Kinchela. The ruffians who shot that brave fellow who lies there were led by Kinchela's agent, Harvey Duff.

ALL Harvey Duff!

Biddy seizes axe. **Mrs O'Kelly** *crosses to fire for poker.* **Donovan** *gets scythe and kneels, sharpening it with stone.*

Tableau.

Molineux first encounters the edge of axe – stepping back, confronts **Mrs O'Kelly** *with the poker, which she flourishes savagely and, crossing in front, eyes with his glass* **Donovan** *sharpening scythe.*

Biddy Harvey Duff sent my only boy across the say!

Donovan I've a long reckoning agin him; but I've kept it warm in my heart.

Mrs O'Kelly An' I've a short one, and there it lies. *(pointing to Conn)*

All Where is he?

Molineux Kinchela and his men are hiding in some den, where they hold Miss O'Neal and Moya prisoners.

All Moya Dolan?

Molineux The niece of your minister – the sweetheart of poor Conn! My men shall aid you in the search; but you are familiar with every hole and corner in the county – you must direct it. Robert Ffolliott awaits you all at Suil-a-beg to lead the hunt – that is, after you have paid your melancholy respects to the Shaughraun.

Mrs O'Kelly No! you could not plaze him betther than to go now. Bring back the news that you have revenged his murder, an' he'll go under the sod wid a light heart.

All Hurroo! To Suil-a-beg! To Suil-a-beg!

*Exeunt rapidly all but **Reilly** and **Sullivan**. **Molineux** gives **Conn** a pinch of snuff; he sneezes. **Reilly** and **Sullivan** turn and watch him off; then rush down.*

26 **Reilly** Sullivan, you must warn Kinchela. Quick! There's not an hour to lose.

Sullivan Where shall I find him?

Conn rises and listens.

Reilly At the Coot's Nest. The lugger came in last night. Tell him to get aboord – take the two women wid him, for he'll have to run for his life.

SULLIVAN Ay, and, bedad, for ours too! If he's caught we're in for it.

Conn creeps to door, and locks it very quietly.

REILLY I feel the rope around my neck.

SULLIVAN The other end is chokin' me.

*As they turn to go they face **Conn**; they stagger back astonished.*

BOTH Murdher, alive!

CONN That's what I am. Murdher, alive, that will live to see you both hanged for it. I'll be at your wake and begorra, I'll give you both a fine character. *(**Sullivan** and **Reilly** rush to the door.)* Asy, boys, asy! The dure is fast an' here's the key. You're in a fine thrap, ho, ho! You made a mistake last night. *(**Sullivan** whispers to **Reilly**.)* Take is asy now.

30

They rush to the table, and each seizes a knife.

REILLY Did ye forget, ma bouchal, that ye're dead?

SULLIVAN *(advancing slowly)* Sure, if we made a mistake last night we can repair it now!

CONN Oh – tare an' ages – what'll I do? *(retreats behind table)*

REILLY We'll just lay you out agin comfortable where you wor. Divil a sowl will be the wiser.

CONN Help! Help!

*Reilly advances and receives the contents of a mug; then **Sullivan**, who gets the plate of snuff in his eyes. **Conn** jumps over the table and makes for the window at back.*

REILLY Screechin' won't save ye! They are miles away by this time.

CONN *(rushing to window and dashing the shutters open)* Help!

Reilly and Sullivan drag Conn back by the hair of his head, and throw him down.

SULLIVAN Shut the windy! I'll quiet him!

Molineux appears at window.

MOLINEUX *(presenting revolver)* Drop those knives! *(a pause)* Do you hear what I said – drop those knives! *(They let their knives fall.)* Now open the door!

CONN There's the key. *(hands it to Reilly doggedly. Reilly unlocks the door. Molineux enters.)* Help me up. *(to Sullivan)* The hangman will do as much for you one day.

Sullivan helps Conn to rise.

MOLINEUX Now! *(Reilly makes a start as if he would escape.)* If you put your head outside the cabin, I'll put a bullet in it! What men are these?

CONN Two of Kinchela's chickens. They know the road we want to thravel.

MOLINEUX Take that. *(hands Conn the revolver)* Do you know how to use it?

CONN I'll thry. *(turns to Sullivan)* What part of the world would you like to be sent to? *(pointing weapon at him)*

MOLINEUX *(drawing his sword and turning to Reilly)* Attention, my friend! Now put your hands in your pockets. *(repeats; Reilly obeys him)* Now take me direct to where your employer, Mr Kinchela, has imprisoned Miss O'Neal; and if on the road you take your hands out of your pockets and attempt to move beyond a reach of my sword, upon my honour as an officer and a gentleman. I shall cut you down! Forward! *(exeunt)*

CONN Attintion! Put your hand in my pocket. *(Sullivan obeys him.)* Now take me straight to where Moya Dolan is shut up; and if ye stir a peg out o' that on the road, by the piper that played before Julius Caesar, I'll save the country six feet of rope. *(They go out.)*

Staging the extract

SET DESIGN

The Victorian theatre was known for its use of lavish scenery and special effects. The original set for *The Shaughraun* would have consisted of large, painted backcloths depicting the Irish coastline, and realistic pieces of scenery that represented locations such as ruined castle walls, the exterior and interior of various cottages, inside a rocky cave and the interior and exterior of a prison. For your own set design you will need to come up with some simple solutions for the staging of the extract.

◆1a Creating the environment

The extract takes place in two settings: outside and then inside Mrs O'Kelly's cottage. The script uses the word "cottage" to refer to the exterior scene and "cabin" to refer to the interior scene. Carry out the following tasks to produce suitable drawings and a set model for the extract.

9

14

- Make a list of the scenic requirements of the extract. For example, the doors, the windows and the furniture.

- Carry out some visual research to find out what the exterior and interior of an Irish peasant cottage would look like. Remember that although the play is set in the mid-1800s, it is quite likely that the cottage would be much older.

- Investigate the uses of a) a composite setting or b) split staging. Decide how you are going to achieve a quick scene change from the outside to the inside of the cottage.

- Experiment with marking-out tape to gauge the size of the space that you will need. The interior scene is quite cluttered because Conn is lying on a shutter and there are tables with food and drink on them as well as a room full of mourners. Work out the dimensions of the room.

PROPS

The extract requires both "personal props" (items that actors carry with them) and "set props" (items that are used on the set). You will need to research what the items that people had available to them between 1840 and 1870 looked like.

◆1b Making a props list

- Go through the script and list the props and where they appear in the extract.

- List the characters in the extract and their personal props from the props list you have created.

- Draw a ground plan of the stage and label it, indicating where each of the set props will be located.

- Provide a drawing or picture of each of the props and label each one with a description and a note of how it is being obtained.

Captain Molineux and Claire Ffolliott in the National Theatre's production (1988)

 COSTUME

Look at the photo on the previous page which shows a scene from a production of the play to give you some idea of the look of the costumes.

◆1c Researching the costumes

1. Refer to the cast list of the extract and copy out the table below. Put no more than two characters on one sheet of A4 paper. Next to each name, supply three pieces of information as a starting point for developing costumes for the play. In column A, insert an image of an item of clothing (e.g. a hat, a shoe, a jacket) that would suit the character and suggest the period (Ireland in the 1840s). In column B, insert an item of clothing that would suggest the status of the character (e.g. rich, poor, clergyman, soldier, peasant farmer, landowner) and in column C, insert a sentence or word that describes the personality of the character (e.g. kind and gentle, devious and untrustworthy).

Characters	A: Period	B: Status	C: Personality
Father Dolan			
Claire Ffolliott			
Mrs O'Kelly			
etc.			

2. Using the list you have made, begin to add other items of clothing for each of the characters that match any one or more of the column headings. In this way, you can build up a wardrobe to suit each of the characters and then put it together to see what it looks like. Because the play is a melodrama, you can exaggerate the use of colour, so that evil characters wear dark colours and good characters wear brighter colours.

 LIGHTING

Lighting in the Victorian theatre up until about 1880 was achieved with gaslight. Gaslight was not as bright as modern electric lighting and was difficult to control. This partly accounts for the exaggerated gestures and mannerisms in the acting and the use of tableau to emphasize points in the action. The two scenes in the extract provide the lighting designer with some interesting challenges.

♦1d Discussion points

Set up a meeting with the production team to discuss how the various design elements of the play will work together. Here are some points to consider:

- How will the difference between the exterior of Scene One and the interior of Scene Two be achieved?

- How will the change in atmosphere between Scene One and Scene Two be created?

- Where are the windows and doors going to be placed and which way will they open?

- Where are the light sources for the scenes?

MUSIC

Music is used in Victorian melodramas in much the same way as it is used in films and television programmes today. It is used to create the mood of a scene or to underscore the action. This kind of music is known as "non-diegetic" music because the audience can hear the music but the characters in the play cannot. Most of the music in *The Shaughraun* works in this way, but in the extract there is also an example of "diegetic" music which is music that is part of the action of the play. This occurs at the opening of the second scene where the keeners are singing the Irish lament "The Oolaghaun" to mourn the death of Conn.

15

Exploring the extract

HISTORICAL AND CULTURAL CONTEXT

As a product of the Victorian era, *The Shaughraun* is significant in that it portrays a situation in Ireland of the late 1860s primarily for an English audience, written by an Irishman working and living in London. The political situation of Ireland seeking independence from British rule is a strong context of the play, and this is apparent through the moral dilemmas faced by the characters. Captain Molineux is the English enemy in the play, but Claire, who is the sister of a known Irish rebel, Robert Ffolliott, finds herself falling in love with him. Conn has assisted in Robert's escape, but Molineux sees the good in him and helps him to rescue the ladies from the grips of the evil Irish landlord, Kinchela.

GENRE AND SUBJECT MATTER

The Shaughraun is an example of Victorian "melodrama". Melodrama was a term originally used to describe a play performed with songs, but by the 19th century it had become associated with a genre that is characterized by action-packed story lines, exaggerated acting, spectacular scenic effects and scenes in which emotions are heightened by the use of music. Most melodramas have recognizable stock characters that are either good or bad, and a plot where evil deeds are exposed and goodness prevails. In many respects, melodrama is very similar to the television soap opera of today.

◆1e **Tableau**

Tableau is used in melodrama to heighten and emphasize the feelings of characters in a scene. In the extract, Biddy (Bridget Madigan), Donovan and Mrs O'Kelly discover that Harvey Duff was responsible for the shooting of Conn. In an earlier scene the audience finds out what Harvey Duff has done when he demands payment from Kinchela by reminding him of his past deeds: *cont...*

17

> HARVEY DUFF Who gave me the office to trap young Ffolliott? Who was it picked out Andy Donovan, an' sent him in irons across the sea, leaving his young wife to die in a madhouse? ... D'ye remember the curse of Bridget Madigan, when her only boy was found guilty on my evidence? (Act Two Scene One)
>
> **17** Read the stage direction that describes the tableau in Scene Two. Create a tableau (or still image) that depicts Biddy brandishing an axe, Mrs O'Kelly carrying a poker and Donovan on one knee sharpening his scythe with a stone. It is important that the gestures and facial expressions strongly express the feelings of each character and show them in an exaggerated way. You may also include Conn laying out dead and Captain Molineux in the tableau as well as the rest of the mourners.

◆1f Thoughts in the head

You can get some idea of how each of the characters feels about Harvey Duff from what he himself says he has done to them and from the three lines each of them says following the tableau. Use the "thoughts in the head" technique to provide you with further evidence about how each of the characters is feeling. Choose someone from the group to act as a "thought director" to tap each performer in the tableau on the shoulder in turn. When each actor is tapped on the shoulder they speak the thoughts of the character aloud. This is an opportunity to say what you really think and feel about Harvey Duff.

Repeat the tableau again after the "thoughts in the head" exercise, with each person showing in their body language and in their facial expression the thoughts they have spoken aloud.

STAGE BUSINESS

18 Look at the section of the script from "REILLY Sullivan, you must warn Kinchela ..." to the end of the extract, and highlight or copy out the stage directions. The movement in this section requires careful choreography if it is to work effectively in performance. You must also pay particular attention to health and safety issues when rehearsing this scene as it involves knives, a gun (fake, of course), Conn being dragged across the floor by his hair and actors having things thrown in their faces. For this reason the scene should be rehearsed in slow motion to begin with and under strict supervision at all times.

◆1g Movement/Forum theatre

Four members of the group volunteer to take on the roles of Conn, Reilly, Sullivan and Molineux. One member of the group volunteers to be the movement director for the scene. The rest of the group is observing the rehearsal process. At any point in the rehearsal, any of the actors or the director can ask for advice from the rest of the group (who act as a forum); equally, anyone from the forum can stop the rehearsal and offer advice or offer to take over one of the roles.

Start rehearsing the scene without the dialogue and concentrate on shifting from one movement point to the next. At this stage the props, such as the mug of drink and the knives, should be mimed. Rehearse the moves of the scene several times to gain "a movement memory" of the scene. Once you have an idea of the movement for the scene, members of the forum can narrate the dialogue from offstage and you can start to fit the movement and dialogue together. At this stage you can start to work with the props and make any adjustments to the timing of moves that may be required. The final stage is to learn the lines for the scene and to rehearse the dialogue, movement and use of props together and to judge the audience's response to the performance.

Exploring characters

STOCK CHARACTERS

The stock characters in a melodrama can be described as one of the following types:

a. hero

b. heroine

c. villain

d. lovable rogue

e. doting parent

f. wronged individuals.

◆1h Character matching by type

Copy out the table below. Read through the extract, decide on the character type of each person and write it next to his or her name. In one play, there can be more than one of any type. For example, write "villain" next to Father Dolan if you think this is the type of stock character he is.

Character	Type	Description
Captain Molineux		
Claire Ffolliott		
Conn		
Mrs O'Kelly		
Robert Ffolliott		
Father Dolan		
Biddy Madigan		
Reilly		
Sullivan		
Donovan		

◆1i Character portraits

The following word portraits describe the first four characters in the above list. Which portrait matches which character from your reading of the extract? Once you have matched the portraits, add any additional descriptions to the list and write your own word portraits for the rest of the characters in the extract. Then check your responses with the answers provided at the end of this section.

Portrait A	Portrait B
headstrong; independent minded; intelligent; witty; impetuous; forgiving	thoughtful; stiff upper lip; romantic; honest; well mannered; pompous
Portrait C	**Portrait D**
foolish; doting; grateful; poor; warm-hearted; feels alone in the world	roguish; energetic; always in trouble; sometimes drunk; likeable; sense of fun

CHARACTER DEVELOPMENT

The characters in a melodrama can sometimes seem two-dimensional, allowing little scope for development. The Irish characters, in particular, in *The Shaughraun* have quite distinct personalities and as actors you need to find ways of showing this in your movement, gestures, use of voice and attitude.

◆1j Role-play

Organization: Work in groups of three, with person A in the role of Mrs O'Kelly, person B as Claire and person C as Father Dolan or a local police officer.

Situation: Mrs O'Kelly and Claire are talking about what good friends Conn (Mrs O'Kelly's son) and Robert (Claire's brother) are. There is a knock at the door and person C enters. He has brought the news that Conn has been shot dead and that Robert has been taken prisoner. Explore the way the characters would respond to this news. cont...

> **Extension:** *Person A leaves the scene to go and see her dead son. Person D (Conn) arrives. Explore the way in which Claire and Father Dolan react to someone who is not dead at all.*

LANGUAGE

A feature in the play is the way in which Boucicault uses dialect words to create authentic Irish characters. Try speaking the following lines in standard English followed by their Irish equivalent and notice the way the pronunciation helps you as an actor to speak with an Irish accent.

English	Irish
… I rolled down and lay as quiet as a sack of potatoes	… I rouled down an' lay as quiet as a sack of pitaties.
Easy, boys, easy! The door is locked and here's the key. You're in a fine trap, ho, ho!	Asy, boys, asy! The dure is fast an' here's the key. You're in a fine thrap, ho, ho!

11

19

◆1k Translation

> Scan through the extract and find more examples of dialect words and phrases, and translate them into standard English to make their meaning clear. Experiment with the sounds of the Irish words and speak the lines in an Irish accent. The educated Irish characters like Robert, Claire and Father Dolan are more difficult to play because they speak standard English but with an Irish accent. Translating standard English words like *you* ("yez") and *old* ("ould") and whole phrases into Irish will help you develop the right accent. Phrases like "be gorra" (*by God*) are useful ways of training the mouth to shape the Irish sounds.

COMPARING TEXTS

From *The Age of Innocence* by Edith Wharton

It was a crowded night at Wallack's Theatre.

The play was *The Shaughraun*, with Dion Boucicault in the title rôle and Harry Montague (Captain Molineux) and Ada Dyas (Claire) as the lovers. The popularity of the admirable English company was at its height, and *The Shaughraun* always packed the house. In the galleries the enthusiasm was unreserved; in the stalls and boxes, people smiled a little at the hackneyed sentiments and clap-trap situations, and enjoyed the play as much as the galleries did.

There was one episode, in particular, that held the house from floor to ceiling. It was that in which Harry Montague, after a sad, almost monosyllabic scene of parting with Miss Dyas, bade her good-bye, and turned to go. The actress, who was standing near the mantelpiece and looking down into the fire, wore a gray cashmere dress without fashionable loopings or trimmings, moulded to her tall figure and flowing in long lines about her feet. Around her neck was a narrow black velvet ribbon with the ends falling down her back.

When her wooer turned from her she rested her arms against the mantel-shelf and bowed her face in her hands. On the threshold he paused to look at her; then he stole back, lifted one of the ends of velvet ribbon, kissed it, and left the room without her hearing him or changing her attitude. And on this silent parting the curtain fell.

◆1| Discussion

This extract is a description of a performance of *The Shaughraun* in New York in 1874. What are the writer's feelings towards the play and how does this come through in the passage? How does the description help to convey a sense of the period and of the acting style?

This is the script for the scene being described in Edith Wharton's novel.

cont...

CLAIRE Don't go.

MOLINEUX Did I hear right? You bid me stay?

CLAIRE Am I mad?

MOLINEUX Miss Ffolliott, I am here.

CLAIRE I forgive you on one condition.

MOLINEUX I accept it, whatever it may be.

CLAIRE Save my brother.

MOLINEUX I'll do my best. Anything else?

CLAIRE Never speak of love to me again.

MOLINEUX Never, never! On my honour I will never breathe a …

CLAIRE Until he is free.

MOLINEUX And then may I – may I – (He stands beside her at fireplace, her head bent down; he steals his arm around her.)

CLAIRE Not a word until then.

MOLINEUX Not a word!

Claire leans her head on his shoulder. Slow close in, as he kisses her.

How does the description of the staged scene differ from the printed script? What does this tell you about the difference between a performance of a play and the script for it?

Answers to tasks 1h and 1i

1h Captain Molineux (a); Claire Ffolliott (b); Conn (d); Mrs O'Kelly (e); Robert Ffolliott (a); Father Dolan (e); Biddy (Bridget) Madigan (f); Reilly (c); Sullivan (c); Donovan (f).

1i Portrait A: Claire; Portrait B: Molineux; Portrait C: Mrs O'Kelly; Portrait D: Conn.

The Importance of Being Earnest

Oscar Wilde

OSCAR WILDE

The Irish playwright, Oscar Fingal O'Flahertie Wills Wilde was born in Dublin on 10 October 1854. He was educated at Trinity College, Dublin, and at Magdalen College, Oxford, where he was awarded a double first in Classics in 1876. Whilst at Oxford he was heavily influenced by the "Art for Art's sake" movement which he developed into his own personal philosophy – "Beauty for Beauty's sake." Whereas his Victorian countryman Dion Boucicault celebrated his Irishness in his plays, Oscar Wilde worked hard in his lifetime at becoming more English than the English. Wilde was a poet, story-writer and playwright and known by all for his sharp wit and wonderful way with words. Here are a few examples:

"Friendship is far more tragic than love. It lasts longer."

"Art is the only serious thing in the world. And the artist is the only person who is never serious."

"In examinations the foolish ask questions that the wise cannot answer."

"To love oneself is the beginning of a life-long romance."

Wilde became notorious in his lifetime for his homosexual relationship with Lord Alfred Douglas that led to his trial for indecent sexual behaviour. He was sentenced to two years hard labour in May 1895, three months after *The Importance of Being Earnest* was performed to great acclaim. On his release from imprisonment he wrote *The Ballad of Reading Gaol,* a poem that expresses all his bitter feelings of being a prisoner. The remaining years of his life were spent in exile in France and Italy and he died in Paris in 1900 having contracted cerebral meningitis.

SUMMARY OF THE PLOT

The plot revolves around the ridiculous circumstances surrounding the name and origins of Jack Worthing. As a baby, his Governess, Miss Prism, mistakenly deposited him in a handbag that she left in the cloakroom of Victoria Station. Jack has grown up not knowing who his real parents are and is best friends with Algernon Moncrieff. Algernon has a cousin, Gwendolen, with whom Jack Worthing is in love. The problem is that Jack is known as Jack in the country and as Ernest in town but Gwendolen only knows Jack in town, so thinks his name is Ernest. Gwendolen is as much in love with his name as she is with the person.

Jack Worthing has a niece in the country called Cecily whom Algernon goes to meet in the guise of being Jack's brother, Ernest, and falls in love with her. Gwendolen has travelled to the country too and thinks that Cecily is a rival in her love for Jack. Both Jack and Algernon are in the situation of being loved for being known as Ernest and arrange to be christened again when Lady Bracknell arrives. This great confusion all works out well in the end. Cecily and Gwendolen become the best of friends and Jack discovers that he is in fact Algernon's elder brother. Lady Bracknell reveals that Jack was named after her brother, Jack's father, who turns out to have been called Ernest, so Gwendolen can marry Ernest (Jack) and Ernest consents to Algernon marrying Cecily.

THE SCENE IN CONTEXT

This scene is at the beginning of the play when Jack has come to town to propose marriage to Gwendolen but has not reckoned on having to deal with her mother, the formidable Lady Bracknell.

The Importance of Being Earnest

By

Oscar Wilde – Ireland

CAST LIST

JOHN WORTHING, J.P. referred to as Jack in the country and Ernest
in town
LADY BRACKNELL mother of Gwendolen
HON. GWENDOLEN FAIRFAX cousin to Algernon

Setting

*Morning-room in **Algernon's** flat in Half-Moon Street, West London. The
room is luxuriously and artistically furnished. Afternoon tea is arranged on
the table.*

Time

The present.

***Gwendolen** has got up to follow her mother and cousin into the music-room
but decides to remain behind with **Jack**, whom she knows as Ernest.*

JACK Charming day it has been, Miss Fairfax.

GWENDOLEN Pray don't talk to me about the weather, Mr Worthing.
Whenever people talk to me about the weather, I always feel
quite certain that they mean something else. And that makes me
so nervous.

JACK I do mean something else.

GWENDOLEN I thought so. In fact, I am never wrong.

JACK And I would like to be allowed to take advantage of Lady Bracknell's temporary absence …

GWENDOLEN I would certainly advise you to do so. Mamma has a way of coming back suddenly into a room that I have often had to speak to her about.

JACK *(nervously)* Miss Fairfax, ever since I met you I have admired you more than any girl … I have ever met since … I met you.

GWENDOLEN Yes, I am quite well aware of the fact. And I often wish that in public, at any rate, you had been more demonstrative. For me you have always had an irresistible fascination. Even before I met you I was far from indifferent to you. *(**Jack** looks at her in amazement.)* We live, as I hope you know, Mr Worthing, in an age of ideals. The fact is constantly mentioned in the more expensive monthly magazines, and has now reached the provincial pulpits, I am told; and my ideal has always been to love some one of the name of Ernest. There is something in the name that inspires absolute confidence. The moment Algernon first mentioned to me that he had a friend called Ernest, I knew I was destined to love you. The name, fortunately for my peace of mind, is, as far as my own experience goes, extremely rare.

JACK You really love me, Gwendolen?

GWENDOLEN Passionately!

JACK Darling! You don't know how happy you've made me.

GWENDOLEN My own Ernest! *(They embrace.)*

JACK But you don't really mean to say that you couldn't love me if my name wasn't Ernest?

GWENDOLEN But your name is Ernest.

JACK Yes, I know it is. But supposing it was something else? Do you mean to say you couldn't love me then?

GWENDOLEN *(glibly)* Ah! that is clearly a metaphysical speculation, and like most metaphysical speculations has very little reference at all to the actual facts of real life, as we know them.

JACK Personally, darling, to speak quite candidly, I don't much care about the name of Ernest ... I don't think the name suits me at all.

GWENDOLEN It suits you perfectly. It is a divine name. It has a music of its own. It produces vibrations.

JACK Well, really, Gwendolen, I must say that I think there are lots of other much nicer names. I think Jack, for instance, a charming name.

GWENDOLEN Jack? ... No, there is very little music in the name Jack, if any at all, indeed. It does not thrill. It produces absolutely no vibrations ... I have known several Jacks, and they all, without exception, were more than usually plain. Besides, Jack is a notorious domesticity for John! And I pity any woman who is married to a man called John. She would have a very tedious life with him. She would probably never be allowed to know the entrancing pleasure of a single moment's solitude. The only really safe name is Ernest.

JACK Gwendolen, I must get christened at once – I mean we must get married at once. There is no time to be lost.

GWENDOLEN Married, Mr Worthing?

JACK *(astounded)* Well ... surely. You know that I love you, and you led me to believe, Miss Fairfax, that you were not absolutely indifferent to me.

GWENDOLEN I adore you. But you haven't proposed to me yet. Nothing has been said at all about marriage. The subject has not even been touched on.

JACK Well ... may I propose to you now?

GWENDOLEN I think it would be an admirable opportunity. And to spare any possible disappointment, Mr Worthing, I think it is only fair to tell you quite frankly beforehand that I am fully determined to accept you.

JACK Gwendolen!

GWENDOLEN Yes, Mr Worthing, what have you got to say to me?

JACK You know what I have got to say to you.

GWENDOLEN Yes, but you don't say it.

JACK Gwendolen, will you marry me? *(Goes on his knees.)*

GWENDOLEN Of course I will, darling. How long have you been about it! I am afraid you have had very little experience in how to propose.

JACK My own one, I have never loved anyone in the world but you.

GWENDOLEN Yes, but men often propose for practice. I know my brother Gerald does. All my girl-friends tell me so. What wonderfully blue eyes you have, Ernest! They are quite, quite blue. I hope you will always look at me just like that, especially when there are other people present.

Enter Lady Bracknell.

LADY BRACKNELL Mr Worthing! Rise, sir, from this semi-recumbent posture. It is most indecorous.

GWENDOLEN Mamma! *(He tries to rise; she restrains him.)* I must beg you to retire. This is no place for you. Besides, Mr Worthing has not quite finished yet.

LADY BRACKNELL Finished what, may I ask?

GWENDOLEN I am engaged to Mr Worthing, mamma. *(They rise together.)*

LADY BRACKNELL Pardon me, you are not engaged to any one. When you do become engaged to some one, I, or your father, should his health permit him, will inform you of the fact. An engagement should come on a young girl as a surprise, pleasant or unpleasant, as the case may be. It is hardly a matter that she could be allowed to arrange for herself ... And now I have a few questions to put to you, Mr Worthing!

JACK I shall be charmed to reply to any questions, Lady Bracknell.

GWENDOLEN You mean if you know the answer to them. Mamma's questions are sometimes peculiarly inquisitorial.

LADY BRACKNELL I intend to make them very inquisitorial. And while I am making these inquiries, you, Gwendolen, will wait for me below in the carriage.

GWENDOLEN *(reproachfully)* Mamma!

LADY BRACKNELL In the carriage, Gwendolen!

*Gwendolen goes to the door. She and **Jack** blow kisses to each other behind **Lady Bracknell**'s back. **Lady Bracknell** looks vaguely about as if she could not understand what the noise was. Finally turns round.*

Gwendolen, the carriage!

GWENDOLEN Yes, mamma. *(Goes out, looking back at **Jack**.)*

LADY BRACKNELL *(sitting down)* You can take a seat, Mr Worthing.

Looks in her pocket for note-book and pencil.

JACK Thank you, Lady Bracknell, I prefer standing.

LADY BRACKNELL *(pencil and note-book in hand)* I feel bound to tell you that you are not down on my list of eligible young men, although I have the same list as the dear Duchess of Bolton has. We work together, in fact. However, I am quite ready to enter your name, should your answers be what a really affectionate mother requires. Do you smoke?

JACK Well yes, I must admit I smoke.

LADY BRACKNELL I am glad to hear it. A man should always have an occupation of some kind. There are far too many idle men in London as it is. How old are you?

JACK Twenty-nine.

LADY BRACKNELL A very good age to be married at. I have always been of opinion that a man who desires to get married should know either everything or nothing. Which do you know?

JACK *(after some hesitation)* I know nothing, Lady Bracknell.

LADY BRACKNELL I am pleased to hear it. I do not approve of

47

anything that tampers with natural ignorance. Ignorance is like a delicate exotic fruit; touch it and the bloom is gone. The whole theory of modern education is radically unsound. Fortunately in England, at any rate, education produces no effect whatsoever. If it did, it would prove a serious danger to the upper classes, and probably lead to acts of violence in Grosvenor Square. What is your income?

JACK Between seven and eight thousand a year.

LADY BRACKNELL *(makes a note in her book)* In land, or in investments?

JACK In investments, chiefly.

LADY BRACKNELL That is satisfactory. What between the duties expected of one during one's lifetime, and the duties exacted from one after one's death, land has ceased to be either a profit or a pleasure. It gives one position, and prevents one from keeping it up. That's all that can be said about land.

JACK I have a country house with some land, of course, attached to it, about fifteen hundred acres, I believe; but I don't depend on that for my real income. In fact, as far as I can make out, the poachers are the only people who make anything out of it.

LADY BRACKNELL A country house! How many bedrooms? Well, that point can be cleared up afterwards. You have a town house, I hope? A girl with a simple unspoiled nature, like Gwendolen, could hardly be expected to reside in the country.

JACK Well, I own a house in Belgrave Square, but it is let by the year to Lady Bloxham. Of course, I can get it back whenever I like, at six months' notice.

LADY BRACKNELL Lady Bloxham? I don't know her.

JACK Oh, she goes about very little. She is a lady considerably advanced in years.

LADY BRACKNELL Ah, nowadays that is no guarantee of respectability of character. What number in Belgrave Square?

JACK 149.

LADY BRACKNELL *(shaking her head)* The unfashionable side. I thought there was something. However, that could easily be altered.

JACK Do you mean the fashion, or the side?

LADY BRACKNELL *(sternly)* Both, if necessary, I presume. What are your politics?

JACK Well, I am afraid I really have none. I am a Liberal Unionist.

LADY BRACKNELL Oh, they count as Tories. They dine with us. Or come in the evening at any rate. You have, of course, no sympathy of any kind with the Radical Party?

JACK Oh! I don't want to put the asses against the classes, if that is what you mean, Lady Bracknell.

LADY BRACKNELL That is exactly what I do mean … ahem! … Are your parents living?

JACK I have lost both my parents.

LADY BRACKNELL Both? … To lose one parent may be regarded as a misfortune … to lose both seems like carelessness. Who was your father? He was evidently a man of some wealth. Was he born in what the Radical papers call the purple of commerce, or did he rise from the ranks of the aristocracy?

JACK I am afraid I really don't know. The fact is, Lady Bracknell, I said I had lost my parents. It would be nearer to the truth to say that my parents seemed to have lost me … I don't actually know who I am by birth. I was … well, I was found.

LADY BRACKNELL Found!

JACK The late Mr Thomas Cardew, an old gentleman of a very charitable and kindly disposition, found me, and gave me the name of Worthing, because he happened to have a first-class ticket for Worthing in his pocket at the time. Worthing is a place in Sussex. It is a seaside resort.

LADY BRACKNELL Where did the charitable gentleman who had a first-class ticket for this seaside resort find you?

JACK *(gravely)* In a hand-bag.

LADY BRACKNELL A hand-bag?

JACK *(very seriously)* Yes, Lady Bracknell. I was in a hand-bag – a somewhat large, black leather hand-bag, with handles to it – an ordinary hand-bag in fact.

LADY BRACKNELL In what locality did this Mr James, or Thomas, Cardew come across this ordinary hand-bag?

JACK In the cloak-room at Victoria Station. It was given to him in mistake for his own.

LADY BRACKNELL The cloak-room at Victoria Station?

JACK Yes. The Brighton line.

LADY BRACKNELL The line is immaterial. Mr Worthing, I confess I feel somewhat bewildered in what you have just told me. To be born, or at any rate bred, in a hand-bag, whether it had handles or not, seems to me to display a contempt for the ordinary decencies of family life that reminds one of the worse excesses of the French Revolution. And I presume you know what that unfortunate movement led to? As for the particular locality in which the hand-bag was found, a cloak-room at a railway station might serve to conceal a social indiscretion – has probably, indeed, been used for that purpose before now – but it could hardly be regarded as an assured basis for a recognised position in good society.

JACK May I ask you then what you would advise me to do? I hardly need to say I would do anything in the world to ensure Gwendolen's happiness.

LADY BRACKNELL I would strongly advise you, Mr Worthing, to try and acquire some relations as soon as possible, and to make a definite effort to produce at any rate one parent, of either sex, before the season is quite over.

JACK Well, I don't see how I could possibly manage to do that. I can produce the hand-bag at any moment. It is in my dressing-room at home. I really think that should satisfy you, Lady Bracknell.

Lady Bracknell Me, sir! What has it to do with me? You can
hardly imagine that I and Lord Bracknell would dream of
allowing our only daughter – a girl brought up with the utmost
care – to marry into a cloak-room, and form an alliance with a
parcel. *(Jack starts indignantly.)* Kindly open the door for me, sir.
You will of course understand that for the future there is to be no
communication of any kind between you and Miss Fairfax.

Lady Bracknell sweeps out in majestic indignation. **Algernon***, from the
other room, strikes up the Wedding March.* **Jack** *looks perfectly furious, and
goes to the door.*

49

50

45

Staging the extract

SET AND PROPS

This scene is set in a stylish apartment of the late Victorian period. It is tastefully furnished and decorated. There is an exit to the Music Room and to the Hallway.

◆2a Staging with style: research

> If you are going to stage the play, particular attention will need to be paid to capturing the period and the style of the furnishings. Oscar Wilde himself was very fond of the work of the Pre-Raphaelite painters, Rossetti and Burne-Jones, and of the interior designer William Morris.
>
> **1.** Research the work of these artists and gather together examples of possible visual ideas for your set design.
>
> **2.** Research antique furniture of the 19th century and put together a visual display of the type of furniture that could appear in the scene.

COSTUME

Wilde was a flamboyant dresser, fond of elegant clothing, and this style is demonstrated through the characters of his plays. Jack and Gwendolen would be wearing the fashionable dress of the 1890s, whilst Lady Bracknell would wear something suiting her older years. The painting opposite, *The Picnic* by James Tissot, was painted in 1875 and shows clothes that are typical of the period.

◆2b Costume design

> From your research, produce costume drawings for the characters in the play. How might you make or obtain these costumes on a limited budget? How might these costumes affect the manner in which the actors move and behave?

Clothes typical of the period, in a painting by James Tissot (1875)

🎧♪ SOUND AND LIGHTING

The sound of horse-drawn carriages going past Algernon's flat could be used to suggest the period of the play. At the end of the scene, Algernon is heard playing Mendelsohn's "Wedding March" on the piano, so you will need to find the music and make a recording of it. The scene takes place in the late afternoon. There is only one lighting state throughout the extract and it will be lit by natural light coming through the windows into the room. The scene needs to be brightly lit to enhance the "lightness" of the mood.

43

Exploring the extract

HISTORICAL AND CULTURAL CONTEXT

The play is an historical record of the manners and behaviour of the upper classes in late Victorian England. Oscar Wilde was holding up a mirror to the very society that would be watching the play and enabling the audience to laugh at themselves. Everything about the play represents a kind of fashion statement of the time. It also shows how people in rich Victorian society spent their time deciding who they should or should not marry. Everything about the play is artificial and it aims to please people with its cleverness. It is far removed from the realities of the everyday life of working people in the late 1890s. The two female characters in the play have very strong personalities but it must be remembered that at the time the play was written women in society did not have the vote and were considered to be second-class citizens.

GENRE AND SUBJECT MATTER

The play is a sophisticated comedy of manners. Every gesture and every word in the play needs to be played with complete seriousness because, for the characters in the play, what they say and do is completely real. For an audience, of course, much of what the characters say and do seems utterly ridiculous. There is a serious point to the play in that Wilde is showing how people in high society can be totally preoccupied with inessential detail and with how much someone is worth. For example, Lady Bracknell is anxious to know which side of Belgrave Square Jack has a house and appears to know that number 149 is on the unfashionable side. Similarly, Lady Bracknell suddenly begins to think that Jack's ward, Cecily, might make Algernon a good wife when she learns from Jack that she is worth £130 000 in investment funds. Whilst it is highly amusing for someone like Jack to be christened again because Gwendolen will only marry a man called Ernest, it does not say much about one person's love for another if they cannot see beyond their Christian name.

◆2c Speaking posh

In order to play the characters and speak Wilde's dialogue, you need to adopt a highly refined voice. Every syllable, every vowel and every consonant that you utter must be articulated and pronounced clearly without any trace of your own accent. Use the following lines to practise speaking in an upper class accent with precise enunciation of each word.

- Pray don't talk to me about the weather, Mr Worthing. Whenever people talk to me about the weather, I always feel quite certain that they mean something else. **35**

- I am pleased to hear it. I do not approve of anything that tampers with natural ignorance. Ignorance is like a delicate exotic fruit; touch it and the bloom is gone. The whole theory of modern education is radically unsound. Fortunately in England, at any rate, education produces no effect whatsoever. If it did, it would prove a serious danger to the upper classes, and probably lead to acts of violence in Grosvenor Square. **39**

- Well, my own dear, sweet, loving little darling, I really can't see why you should object to the name of Algernon. It is not at all a bad name. In fact, it is rather an aristocratic name. Half of the chaps who get into the Bankruptcy Court are called Algernon. But seriously, Cecily … if my name was Algy, couldn't you love me?

- Under an assumed name he drank, I've just been informed by my butler, an entire pint bottle of my Perrier-Jouet, Brut, '89; wine I was specially reserving for myself. Continuing his disgraceful deception, he succeeded in the course of the afternoon in alienating the affections of my only ward. He subsequently stayed to tea, and devoured every single muffin. And what makes his conduct more heartless is, that he was perfectly well aware from the first that I have no brother, that I never had a brother, and that I don't intend to have a brother, not even of any kind. I distinctly told him so myself yesterday afternoon.

Exploring characters

JACK

There is no doubt that Jack is head-over-heels in love with Gwendolen. In the scene he has come prepared to get down on one knee and propose to the woman he wishes to marry. He is somewhat surprised by the forward way in which Gwendolen behaves and is even more angered by Lady Bracknell's refusal to allow him to marry her daughter.

◆2d Hot-seating

The following hot-seating exercise is designed to start you thinking about the role of Jack, and how the other characters in the play relate to him. The person in the hot seat must answer the questions asked of him/her in the role of Jack, which means they need to think and behave like Jack. You can use lines, or words and phrases from the play to answer the questions if they are appropriate. When all of the questions from the group have been asked and answered, the person who has been in the hot seat tells the rest of the group what it felt like to be in the role of Jack.

Starter questions to Jack:

- Why don't you tell Gwendolen that your name is really Jack?
- What can you do to persuade Lady Bracknell that you are a suitable husband for her daughter?

GWENDOLEN AND LADY BRACKNELL

Later in the play, one of the characters observes that, "All women become like their mothers. That is their tragedy. No man does. That's his." and there are signs that Gwendolen is a younger version of her mother in the way that she is single-minded about things. However,

Gwendolen is enjoying the romance of the situation whereas Lady Bracknell is more concerned about how it will appear to her society friends if her daughter marries "into a cloak-room" because Jack, as a baby, was found in a left-luggage office.

◆2e **Role-play**

1. *Organization:* Work with a partner. One of you takes on the role of Lady Bracknell and the other is her friend, the Duchess of Bolton.

   Situation: Lady Bracknell confides in her friend the details of her interview with Jack.

   Opening line: **LADY BRACKNELL:** *My dear Duchess, you will scarcely believe what I have to tell you!*

2. *Organization:* Work in a group of three or four. One is a reporter from *Hello!* or *OK!* magazine. The others take on roles as Lady Bracknell, Gwendolen and Jack Worthing.

   Situation: Jack (or Ernest) and Gwendolen are now engaged, and have agreed to be interviewed.

   Opening Line: **REPORTER:** *Miss Fairfax, what first attracted you to your fiancé?*

   Extension: Create a series of tableaux or still pictures, which could represent photographs accompanying the magazine article.

   Points to consider: Don't forget to include remarks that display Lady Bracknell's concern for her status in society. How will you create a contrast between the informality of the interviewer and the more formal speech of the other characters?

3. What does this exercise show you about the similarities and differences between the mother and daughter? Try to identify aspects of how they speak as well as what they say and do. How does this exercise help you to understand the difference in attitude towards marriage between Gwendolen and Lady Bracknell? In what ways does Jack behave differently towards the two women?

GWENDOLEN

At the end of the scene, Lady Bracknell goes off to tell Gwendolen what she thinks of Jack and forbids Gwendolen from marrying him.

43

◆2f Narrating

> **1.** Imagine that Gwendolen, in the role of a Narrator, is retelling the offstage scene between her and her mother, Lady Bracknell. Write and perform the narration for Gwendolen. Try to imitate Wilde's style of writing.
>
> **2.** How does your narration help you to show Gwendolen's attitude to Jack and Lady Bracknell? What does your narration demonstrate about Gwendolen's character?

COMPARING TEXTS

Look at this painting called *The Proposal* by Alfred W. Elmore. It was painted around the same time as the play was written. How does its portrayal of a marriage proposal differ from that in the play?

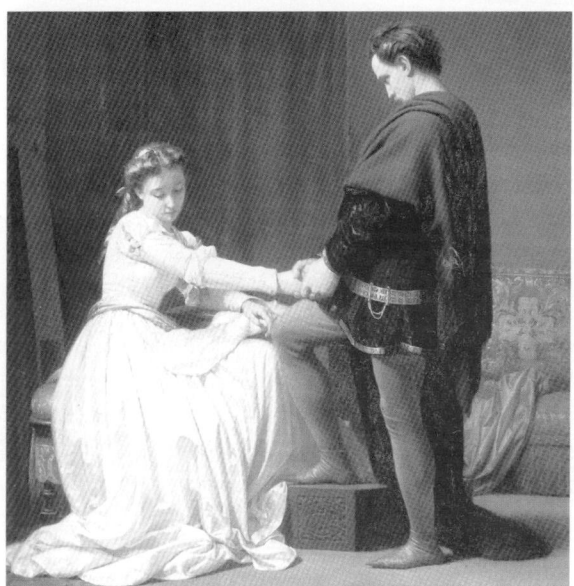

◆2g Still image and devised work

Organization: Work in a group of four. Two people will portray the characters in the painting and the other two will be their voices.

Task: **1.** Set up a still image that is a near copy of the situation in the picture and devise a line of dialogue for the two characters that will be spoken offstage like a soundtrack.

2. Set up a further two still images, one to depict the positioning and attitude of the two people two or three minutes *before* the moment in the painting, and one to depict the moment several minutes *after* the moment in the painting.

3. Create the lines of dialogue for these further still images and show your three images with their soundtrack of dialogue to the rest of the class. What does each group's portrayal of the painting tell you about the characters and their feelings about each other?

Extension: Use this work as a starting point for your own piece of devised work. You can invent additional characters and scenes to tell your story and use the moment captured in the painting at any point in your play.

This extract is from *The Love Letters of Ragie Patel* written by Lee Hall. The young man and young woman in this scene are discussing their forthcoming arranged marriage.

RAMESH I'm sorry about your Dad. I didn't mean this to get into some kind of argument.

NANDINI It wasn't your fault.

RAMESH You know, it's quite weird for me as well.

NANDINI But you want to get married don't you?

RAMESH Of course.

NANDINI Then why is it weird?

RAMESH Well, I've never done it before.

NANDINI Do you believe in all this?

RAMESH All what?

NANDINI Everything being arranged like this. You don't even know me.

RAMESH Well, that's why I came up. To get to know you. Look, I don't want to make you do something you don't want to do.

NANDINI You're not making me do anything.

RAMESH It's just … Well, there's plenty of people who get married because they think they're in love at 18 or 19 and then they're divorced by the time they're 25. This way it's safer.

NANDINI Safer?

RAMESH You know what you're getting into.

NANDINI But you might not even like me.

RAMESH I do like you. I can see that already.

NANDINI You've only just met me. You don't know what I'm really like.

RAMESH I can see you're a very nice person.

NANDINI You don't know that I am though, do you?

RAMESH But you can get a feeling.

NANDINI But you can't tell what goes on in people's lives, can you?

RAMESH Look, I'm not trying to be funny or anything. But you seem very special.

NANDINI What's special about me?

RAMESH You're your own woman. I like that. And …

NANDINI And?

RAMESH You're very beautiful.

NANDINI Please.

RAMESH Look, I wouldn't marry you just because I had to. I'd have to like you. And I think there's some chemistry between us.

NANDINI Chemistry?

RAMESH Don't you think? Have you ever kissed anyone?

NANDINI A bit.

RAMESH You know, I think you're gorgeous.

NANDINI Look, I don't know what I think about all this.
I know you're a very decent man and everything. It's just
… didn't you ever want to fall in love properly?

◆2h Discussion

⊂⊃ ⊂⊃

1. How does the relationship between Ramesh and Nandini compare to that of Jack and Gwendolen?

2. Arranged marriages are the accepted norm in many cultures and religions. What advantages and disadvantages do they have over the kind of marriage agreement that is being negotiated in *The Importance of Being Earnest?*

A Respectable Wedding

Bertolt Brecht

BERTOLT BRECHT

Brecht was born in 1898 in the South German town of Augsburg, the son of a prosperous paper factory director. During World War I he was drafted into the army as a medical orderly and in 1918 he wrote *Baal*, his first successful play. In 1922 he married his pregnant girlfriend, Marianne Zoff, but they divorced in 1927. Brecht is as well known for his ideas about theatre practice as he is as a playwright. Of his 40 or so plays, the most frequently performed are *The Caucasian Chalk Circle* (1945), *The Threepenny Opera* (1928) and *Mother Courage* (1939).

Brecht believed that the theatre was a place where audiences could be made to think and to realize that they could change the capitalist society in which they lived. Brecht developed the "epic theatre" form, which uses "alienation" or distancing effects to remind the audience that they are watching a play. By using devices like songs, projected titles and characters speaking directly to the audience, Brecht wanted to make sure that the audience was not completely absorbed in the drama. This was so that the audience could remain objective and critical about what was happening in the play and why it was happening.

Brecht was on Hitler's death-list and was forced to flee Nazi Germany in 1933. After travelling across Europe and Russia, he arrived with his family in the United States in 1941. In 1947 he was called to account for his Marxist beliefs before Senator McCarthy's UnAmerican Activities Committee. Brecht then returned to live in Soviet-occupied East Berlin and formed the Berliner Ensemble with his second wife, Helene Weigel. He died in 1956.

SUMMARY OF THE PLOT

The plot consists of a family sitting down for a meal at the wedding reception of the recently-married Bride and Groom. The happiest day of a young couple's life is turned into something of a disaster when the furniture around them starts to collapse and some of the wedding guests fall out with each other.

THE SCENE IN CONTEXT

The extract takes place half way through the play. The Guests have already eaten the main course, the Young Man has given a speech wishing the married couple a happy life together and the Father has been embarrassing everyone with his long and boring stories. The extract starts with them sitting back down at the table after a dance. When the table was moved to make space for the dancing one of its legs went askew, and the sofa cracked when the Wife and the Friend sat down on it. At the start of the extract, the Wife is sitting next to the Groom and the Mother is offstage in the kitchen preparing the next course.

After the end of the extract, the Bride and Groom are glad to be left alone and start to take each other's clothes off. The Groom drags his Bride into the bedroom and minutes later we hear the sound of the bed collapsing under the weight of their lovemaking.

A Respectable Wedding

By

Bertolt Brecht – Germany
(translated by Jean Benedetti)

75 ## CAST LIST

(BRIDEGROOM'S) FRIEND
(BRIDEGROOM'S) MOTHER
BRIDE
HUSBAND
WIFE
YOUNG MAN
(BRIDE'S) FATHER
(BRIDE'S) SISTER
BRIDEGROOM

Setting

*A whitewashed room with a large rectangular table in the middle. A red paper lantern over it. Nine plain, wide wooden armchairs. Against the back wall, R., a sofa. L., a cupboard. A curtained door between them. Upstage L., a low coffee table and two chairs. L., a door; R., a window. Tables, chairs, and cupboards are in unpolished natural wood. It is evening. The red lamp is alight. The **wedding guests** are at the table, eating.*

*The **Sister**, the **Bride**, and the **Young Man** come in.*

SISTER We've been helping Mother with the blancmange.

GROOM Doesn't matter. We're all in excellent form here. We've been swapping stories.

78 **YOUNG MAN** It's going to be a smashing blancmange.

56

WIFE Made it on the cooker, did you?

SISTER No. Blancmange is never made on the cooker in this house.

WIFE I only thought you'd say you made it on the cooker because the two of you have got such red faces. *(Laughs and drops into a chair.)* Oh! *(Gets up.)*

FRIEND Was that something going?

WIFE Oh dear, the chair …

GROOM It can't have. You can bounce about on that as much as you like. Two-inch pegs, I used.

WIFE I'm not going to risk sitting on it any more. I'll sit on the sofa.

SISTER You've already sat there. A leg's come off.

FRIEND *(feeling under her chair)* There really is something wrong here. It isn't a splinter this time. But better watch out for your clothes.

GROOM *(coming across)* I didn't realize it was that one, or I'd have asked you to sit somewhere else.

BRIDE Then it would have been that one.

HUSBAND Here's one going begging.

Mother comes in. 68

MOTHER Here's the blancmange. And the mulled claret.

FRIEND Splendid. Mulled claret. *(He sprawls in his chair.)* That was just one of the arms. And I haven't torn anything. Let's have a drink. *(The arm of the chair is broken.)*

GROOM That's more like it. Cheers.

ALL Cheers.

GROOM And here's to you, Mother.

MOTHER Don't splash your nice waistcoat with the wine. There's a spot on it already. 78

FATHER Talking of chairs … Rosenberg and Co. used to have chairs for the customers in their office with the seats so low your knees came up to your chin. You felt so much at home that Rosenberg and Co. got rich on it. He got a better place and better fittings, but he kept the chairs. He used to say in a very emotional way, 'That's the kind of simple furniture I started out with. May God punish me for my pride if I ever forget it.'

WIFE I didn't ask your chairs to break. It's not my fault.

HUSBAND No one said it was.

WIFE That's just it. You want to put me in the wrong.

FRIEND I detect a discordant note. Shall I get my guitar and sing something?

GROOM Aren't you tired?

FRIEND What from?

GROOM Dancing, drinking. With your stomach trouble.

FRIEND I have not got stomach trouble.

GROOM You're always taking bicarbonate of soda.

FRIEND That doesn't make me ill by a long chalk.

GROOM It was only in your own interest.

FRIEND Thanks, but I'm not tired.

Pause.

YOUNG MAN Have you been to see that play Baal?

HUSBAND Yes; it's a load of filth.

YOUNG MAN A lot of punch in it, though.

HUSBAND All right: so it's a load of filth with punch in it. That's worse than having none. It's no excuse for a man to say that he's got a gift for writing filth. Filth should be kept off the stage.

Pause.

FATHER Those modern writers are always dragging family life in the   78
mud. When it's the best thing we Germans have.

FRIEND True enough.

Pause.

GROOM Well. Now cheer up, everyone. I don't get married every
day. Drink up, and don't sit there like a lot of stiffs. Look, I'm
going to take my coat off. *(He does so.)*

Pause.

FRIEND Got any cards? We might play pontoon.

GROOM They're in the cupboard.

WIFE Which won't open.

FRIEND You might do it with a crowbar.

BRIDE Be serious.

FRIEND Well, you'll have to get it open some time.

BRIDE But not today.

GROOM Just to get a few cards out.

FRIEND *(rudely)* All right, then you tell us just what else one can do   78
in this place.

WIFE It might be the moment to look at the rest of the furniture.

GROOM That's an idea. I'll lead the way.

All get up.

SISTER I think I'll go on sitting here.

BRIDE All by yourself? You can't.

SISTER Why not?

BRIDE Because there are limits.

SISTER Then let me tell you I didn't want to get up because the chair's bust.

BRIDE How did you bust it?

SISTER It just went.

FRIEND *(feeling the chair)* As long as you take care and sit down gently it won't matter.

FATHER Perhaps we could go and look at the rest of the furniture now.

FRIEND *(quietly to the **Wife**)* The table's still intact.

GROOM They're nothing special really …

WIFE So long as they hold up.

GROOM Come on, Maria.

BRIDE *(stays seated)* I'll be along in a minute. You go on.

All leave through the centre door. As they go:

WIFE *(to the **Friend**)* The bridegroom's taken his jacket off.

FRIEND That's rash of him. No holds barred now.

*The **Bride** sits at the table and snivels.*

GROOM I must go and look for the torch; something's wrong with the wiring.

BRIDE Why didn't you get a proper electrician to do it?

GROOM What's the matter with you? I didn't care for the way your sister behaved, either.

BRIDE How about your friend?

GROOM That's no way to dance if you want to keep people's respect.

BRIDE And Mildner too. All that stuff about the pure young bride was deliberate. I went all red, and everybody noticed. He kept staring at me, too. And then that awful song. He's been getting his own back for something.

GROOM Those dirty jokes. All because he thought you're the sort of person it doesn't matter with.

BRIDE Don't forget he's your friend. And I'm not that sort of person.

GROOM How can we get rid of them? There they are, stuffing themselves, smoking, chattering away; they just don't want to go. After all it's our party.

BRIDE A nice party!

GROOM Don't act that way. Once they've gone …

BRIDE They've spoilt everything now.

GROOM I wish we were alone. Here they are.

BRIDE I don't want them to go. That'll be even worse.

GROOM (*puts his coat on again quickly*) It's chillier than I thought.

*The **others** appear in the door.*

FATHER We had to wait in the kitchen as the bedroom light wasn't working.

FRIEND Are we intruding?

*The **Wife** has a fit of laughter.*

HUSBAND What is it now?

WIFE It's so funny.

HUSBAND What's funny?

WIFE Everything. Everything. The broken chairs, the home-made furniture. The entertainment. (*laughs horribly*)

Bride Emmy, really!

73

Wife All broken. *(Laughing, she drops into a chair which breaks.)* There goes another. There goes another. Now I'll have to sit on the floor.

Friend *(joins in the laughter)* That's a fact. We ought to have brought camp stools.

Husband *(grabs his Wife)* You must be ill. If you go around behaving like that and the furniture breaks it won't be the furniture's fault. *(to the Groom)* I'm sorry.

Friend Let's sit down as best we can. So long as we keep cheerful that's all that counts.

They sit.

Sister A pity we couldn't see. The beds are really very nice.

Wife No, the light didn't work either.

Bride Won't you fetch some more wine, Jacob?

Groom It's in the cellar. Let's have the key.

Bride Just a moment.

They go out.

Wife There's a peculiar smell here too.

Friend It didn't seem to be there before.

Sister I don't smell anything.

Wife I know what it is. It's the glue.

Friend That's why they wanted that eau-de-Cologne I gave them. An entire half bottle.

Wife But the smell of the glue's coming through; there's no hiding it now.

*The **Bride** returns.*

FATHER You're a pretty sight, standing in the door like that. You   73
always were pretty to look at, even as a child. But now you're
blooming.

WIFE That's a well-cut frock.

BRIDE No camouflage needed, thank God.

WIFE Was that aimed at anybody?

BRIDE If the cap fits.

WIFE People who live in glass houses shouldn't throw stones.

BRIDE And who's in a glass house?

WIFE That frock's a very good piece of work, because no one would
imagine you were …

FRIEND Cheers. Fine wine, that.   73

BRIDE *(crying)* That's that's …

HUSBAND What's all this about?

GROOM *(returns)* Here's the wine. What's the matter with you?

SISTER A remark in bad taste.

FATHER Calm down now. Cheers.

GROOM *(to the **Sister**)* You're not to insult our guests.

SISTER But the guests can insult your wife.   78

WIFE I never said a thing.

HUSBAND Oh yes you did. You were offensive.

WIFE *(annoyed)* I only spoke the truth.

GROOM And what truth was that?

WIFE Be your age.

Husband *(leaning towards her)* Just you control yourself.

Wife When a woman's pregnant she's pregnant.

*The **Husband** rips a leg from the table and throws it at his **Wife**, but it hits a vase on top of the cupboard. The **Wife** cries.*

Groom *(angrily, to the **Sister**)* That was the vase you gave us.

Sister You can't have thought much of it, or you wouldn't have put it up there.

Groom I've no time to argue with you now, because it was my table as well.

(He feels to see if it will hold up.)

Husband *(walks agitatedly up and down)* There: I've lifted a hand to her. So now I'm the brute. It's always the same story: she's the martyr, I'm the brute. Seven years I've put up with it, and you may well ask who made a brute of me. My hands were always too tired from working for her to be able to hit her. If I'm on top of the world she's got a pain; if I have a drink she counts the pennies; but if I count the pennies she bursts into tears. Once I had to throw out a picture I was very fond of, because she disliked it. She disliked it because I was fond of it. When I had thrown it out she picked it up and hung it in her room. As soon as I saw it there she was happy and said, 'It's good enough for me.' Then she was sorry for herself for being reduced to picking up my throw-outs. I got angry and took it off her, and then she cried because she couldn't even have that. 'Not even that' was her phrase, even when it was something we couldn't possibly afford. But that's the way she is, and that's the way they all are. As soon as the wedding's over you're no longer a beast working for its mistress, you're a man working for a beast; and it drags you down till there's nothing you don't deserve.

Pause.

Groom *(with an effort)* Have something more to drink? It's only nine.

FRIEND We've run out of chairs.

YOUNG MAN We could still dance.

FRIEND I've had enough of that.

GROOM You liked it earlier on all right.

FRIEND I hadn't got the splinter.

GROOM Oh, I see. *(laughs)* Is that why you've been standing in that subdued way?

FRIEND It wasn't my chair, was it?

GROOM No, it was mine. Was. Now it isn't any more.

FRIEND Then we may as well go. *(goes out)*

YOUNG MAN Thank you. That was very nice. But it's time for me to put my coat on.

WIFE Take me home.

HUSBAND *(goes out and comes back with his **Wife**'s things)* And I must apologize again for this wife of mine.

GROOM You don't have to.

WIFE I daren't go home.

HUSBAND That's your revenge. But the play-acting's all over now, and we're coming to the serious bit. *(takes her arm)* Off we go. *(He leaves with his **Wife**, who is silent and dejected.)*

GROOM Now they've gorged they're anxious to get away. After that we'll be on our own, with half the evening to fill.

BRIDE A moment ago you were longing for them to get out. One never knows where one is with you, does one? And of course you don't love me, either.

FRIEND *(comes back with his hat on. Spitefully)* The stink has become almost unbearable.

GROOM What stink?

FRIEND That glue that wouldn't stick. I call it cheek asking people to such a rubbish dump.

GROOM Then you'd better forgive me for not appreciating your dirty song and having let you break my chair.

FRIEND Why don't you wait for your nuptial dropsy bed? I wish you a very good night. *(goes)*

GROOM Go to hell.

FATHER I think we'd better go too. We can talk about the furniture another time, and the beds are there if you want them. I thought it'd be a help if I told stories that had no connection with the company. It's always a mistake to leave people to their own devices. Come along, Ina.

SISTER It's a pity such a nice evening should end like this. After all, you only have it once. Life begins tomorrow, as Hans says.

BRIDE You did your best to contribute. And just how long have you been calling Herr Mildner Hans?

YOUNG MAN Thanks again. I thought it was a very nice evening.

All three go.

GROOM Thank God they've gone at last.

BRIDE Yes: to spread our disgrace all over town. I don't know how I can face it. Tomorrow they'll all know what happened. And how they'll laugh. They'll sit sniggering behind their windows. They'll stare at us in church as they think of the furniture and the lights that wouldn't work and the blancmange that went wrong, and, to cap it all, that the bride was pregnant. And there was I going to say the baby was premature.

GROOM What about the furniture too? Five month's work! Have you thought of that? They only pissed themselves laughing over that dirty song because you'd danced with them as if you were in a whorehouse, till all the best chairs were bust. A friend of yours, she was.

BRIDE And it was a friend of yours who sang that song. To hell with your furniture. It isn't even stained, because you said the look didn't matter so long as it was solid and comfortable. Five months wasted while you got it finished, and by then I was showing. This rubbish, this trash, this shoddy workmanship. What on earth did we get married for?

GROOM Well, they've gone now, and this is the start of our wedding night. This is it.

Staging the extract

⚔ SET AND PROPS

The play can be set at the time it was written (in the 1920s) or at any time since. The period can be suggested by the look of the furniture and the props. The intriguing design aspect of the play is that the Bridegroom has made all the furniture and most of it starts to collapse because he has also made his own glue, which becomes unstuck. This provides a real opportunity for creative design ideas. The extract requires a considerable number of props because the characters are all eating and drinking to celebrate the wedding.

♦3a **Props list**

Go through the extract and mark all the references in the stage directions and in the dialogue to any items that are needed. For example, the Mother enters with blancmange and mulled claret. From this you need to draw the conclusion that nine people are going to be eating and drinking and will require bowls, glasses and cutlery. Once you have marked up the script, copy out the following table and make a props list for the extract.

Prop number	Description	Notes
1	tray with bowl of blancmange and bowl of mulled claret	These are carried in by the Mother
2 etc		

57

◆3b Ground plan

1. Look at the description of the setting and the photograph of a British production of the play on the next page. This will give you some ideas about how to stage the scene but you can change the setting to suit your own production.

2. Draw a 1:25 scale ground plan of the setting that shows:
   - how you are going to stage the play in your performance space. Will it be end-on, in-the-round, traverse?
   - the position of the audience in relation to the performance space
   - the entrance/exit. There needs to be one at least one door off to the rest of the house.
   - the position of the furniture.

 ## COSTUME

The costume for the play is relatively straightforward as all the guests are wearing their smart dresses and suits for a wedding. The Bride's costume is the most specialist form of clothing but if you set the play in the present day then you could look at catalogues of bridal wear to give you some design ideas.

◆3c Specific costumes

Look at the production photograph of the play on the next page. The characters are sitting around the table in the following positions:

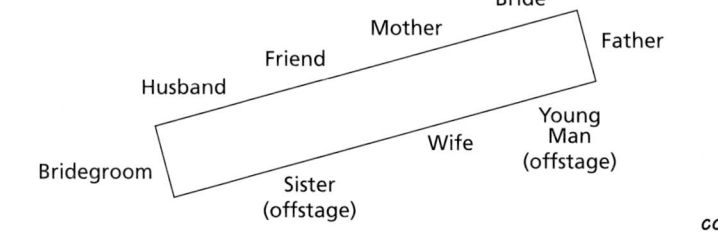

cont...

Write a list detailing what each character is wearing. What do the clothes say to you about the characters? How do the costumes show the differences in age of the characters? What colours are the clothes? Use this information as the starting point for your own research and costume designs.

A scene from the 1978 production at Open Space Theatre, London, directed by Mike Okrent

 LIGHTING

The lighting for the play requires the room to be lit in a naturalistic way. You will need to determine the source of natural lighting in the play and the time of day. There should be a window somewhere in the room and some electric lighting that will be the main sources of light. As there is something wrong with the electricity, the lights can flicker on and off at some point. The stage direction suggests the use of a red paper lantern over the table. What effect will this create?

♪ SOUND

The sound requirements for the play are minimal, but they could help to suggest the setting by the use of quiet background sounds. For example, the sound of traffic would suggest that the family live in a house in town, whereas the sound of birdsong would suggest the country. You might also consider reinforcing the sound of the breaking furniture in some way.

Exploring the extract

HISTORICAL AND CULTURAL CONTEXT

The play was first performed in 1926 and was written as a parody of German society of the day. Weddings are a feature in most societies and are a happy occasion, celebrating the union of a man and a woman as they declare their love for one another in a very public way. Traditionally, one of the purposes of marriage is to form a legal bond between a man and a woman, providing a solid foundation upon which to raise a family. Because of this, it was often assumed that the woman would be a virgin when she married. The title of Brecht's play is deliberately ironic since the behaviour of some of the guests is far from respectable. Earlier in the play, the Friend sings a vulgar song about a "Groom-to-be" going to a prostitute to satisfy his desire rather than having sex before marriage, whilst the "Bride-to-be" satisfies her desire with "a solid chap who simply didn't care". The Groom's Sister flirts unashamedly with the Young Man and the Wife reveals to everyone that the Bride is, in fact, pregnant.

◆3d **Discussion and writing**

- What does "being married" mean to you?
- Should a man and a woman be married *before* they have children? If so, why?
- Describe a wedding you have been to and discuss the sorts of rituals that went on. How did you feel about being at the wedding? What was your role? What purpose did it serve for those involved?
- Imagine that you were one of the guests at the wedding of Brecht's play. Write a letter to a friend or relation telling them what happened and how you felt about it. The point of view will differ depending upon which character you choose to be.

GENRE AND SUBJECT MATTER

This is a very early play by Brecht, written before 1920, and is a fairly conventional, realistic comedy. The treatment of the subject matter shows all the hallmarks of his later work in the way that he portrays the hypocrisy of the middle classes. The whole play is an ironic joke in that Brecht is turning the idea of marriage on its head. Marriages are supposed to be built on firm foundations but the marriage in the play seems doomed from the start, signified by the collapse of the furniture. At the end of the play, when the Bride and Groom go to bed, this too is heard crashing to the floor offstage.

◆3e What's funny?

Much of the comedy in the play arises from the embarrassing things that the characters say about each other or through their ridiculous behaviour. Some of the comedy will be visual (for example, the breaking of a chair leg), and some will be verbal (for instance, when the Wife in her anger reveals that the Bride is pregnant and the Friend tries to change the subject by saying, "Cheers. Fine wine, that."). There are also moments when the comic effect is achieved through both visual and verbal means.

62

64

63

1. Go through the script and decide which moments you think the audience will find funny.

2. Mark the moments of visual comedy with 🙂 and the moments of verbal comedy with 💬.

◆3f Comedy is a serious business

The comedy needs to be played through the characters in a realistic and believable way. Acting the play for laughs is not the way to achieve this. The more serious the characters, the funnier the play will be.

1. *Task:* Reread the section that begins:

   FATHER: You're a pretty sight, standing in the door like that …
   and ends:
   The **Husband** *rips a leg from the table and throws it at his* **Wife**, *but it hits a vase on top of the cupboard. The* **Wife** *cries.* *cont…*

63

2. Act out this scene by "sending up" the characters. Make your acting exaggerated and speak the lines as though you think they are all funny.

3. Act out the scene again, but this time play the characters realistically. Speak the dialogue as though you really mean what you are saying.
   - What differences do you notice between the two styles of playing?
   - Which approach is more appropriate for the genre of the play and why?

Exploring characters

In the cast list and in the speech headings, Brecht avoids giving the characters actual names and instead just refers to them in terms of their relationship to the Bride and Groom.

56

♦3g Who's who? 1

As with most weddings, some of the guests in the play are the friends and relations of the Bride and some are those of the Groom.

Organization: Draw two columns on a sheet of paper. Head the first column "Bride" and the second column "Groom".

Task: Read through the play and work out which characters the Groom invited and which the Bride invited. Write the Bride's guests in the first column and the Groom's guests in the second. Anyone invited by both characters can appear in both columns.

Extension: Discuss your list with a partner, or in a small group, and note any differences. Decide on a final list.

♦3h Who's who? 2

Some of the characters' actual names are revealed through the dialogue:

Maria   Ina   Hans Mildner   Jacob   Emmy

Organization: Work in small groups.

Task: Read through the play and find the names above. Decide which five of the nine characters have these names. Note down any evidence that supports your decision to assign a name to a particular character. Present your findings to the rest of your class, giving reasons for your group's decision. Listen to any arguments from other groups in the class and make a final decision as a result.

(The correct answers can be found at the end of this section.)

BRIDE AND GROOM

The Bride should be the centre of attention on her wedding day and be truly happy. This is not exactly the case in this play. Brecht's Bride is not happy about the Groom's Friend because he sings smutty songs, and the Groom is showing signs of jealousy because of the way his new wife was dancing with the Friend. This is just the beginning of the uneasy relationship between the Bride and the Groom.

◆3i Hot-seating

Organization: Groups of five or six.

Task: One person takes the role of the Bride and sits on a chair facing the rest of the group, each of whom is in the role of the Groom. Members of the group take turns to ask the Bride questions related to the situation in the play – the person playing the Bride must answer in character.

Extension: Repeat the exercise, this time with one person as the Groom sitting on the "hot-seat". The rest of the group take the role of the Bride.

Sample questions for the Bride:

- Why did you agree to marry me?
- Are you going to flirt with all my friends?
- Will you be a good cook and look after me like my mother does?
- Are we doing the right thing, keeping the baby?
- Will we have to see much of your father now that we're married?
- Do you love me?

Sample questions to the Groom:

- Does your mother always have to fuss over you?
- Why can't we go out and buy some proper furniture?
- Did you marry me just because I'm pregnant?
- Did you know that your so-called friend was flirting with me?
- Why did you let that woman speak to me like that?
- Do you love me?

HUSBAND AND WIFE

The Husband and Wife have been married for seven years and the Husband sums up what married life has been like for him when he says, "As soon as the wedding's over you're no longer a beast working for its mistress, you're a man working for a beast; and it drags you down till there's nothing you don't deserve." In other words, Brecht uses this couple to show what he believes marriage can become – they are a projection of the possible future life of the Bride and Groom. In many ways, the Husband is represented as being under his wife's thumb, and she drives him to the point where he loses his temper and throws a table leg at her. Equally, the Wife is represented in a stereotypical way – she is unkind to the other women in the play and constantly nags and criticizes her husband.

♦3j **Role-play**

This exercise is about exploring the relationship between the Husband and Wife. The Wife probably wants to go to the wedding reception to gloat about the Bride being pregnant, whereas the Husband is going out of a sense of duty and to make sure that his Wife behaves herself.

Organization: Work in groups of three or four. Person A is the Wife, Person B is the Husband. Persons C and D are the directors of an improvization. Persons C and D can stop the improvization at any time and make suggestions about what Person A or B is saying or doing, or take over one of the roles to give the actor the responsibility of directing them. All the feedback and discussion between the actors and directors should be positive and focus on creating two believable and truthful characters.

Situation: The Husband and Wife are getting ready for the wedding in their own home. The Husband has lost one of his socks and the Wife is putting on her make-up. The time is 11.30 a.m. and the wedding is at one o'clock.

Starting lines: HUSBAND: Have you seen what time it is, woman?
WIFE: I'm almost ready, which is more than I can say for you.

THE OTHER WEDDING GUESTS

◆3k Thoughts in the head

Organization: Work in groups of ten or more. Look at the seating plan in exercise 3c. Arrange the nine characters around a table in the same seating positions. You will need to decide where the Sister and the Young Man are sitting. One or more people are going to act as "thought directors". Their role will be to tap any of the characters on the shoulder at which point the character will speak their thoughts about one of the other characters. Remember that we often think things about other people that we would not say out aloud, so use this opportunity to say what you *really* think about another character.

Task: Use the information in the table below to focus on different characters at different moments in the play. Each character hears what the other characters think about them but do not speak their thoughts at that point.

What are my thoughts about the ...	Moment in the play
Friend?	when he says, "All right, then you tell us just what else one can do in this place."
Young Man?	when he returns with the Sister and says, "It's going to be a smashing blancmange."
Sister	when she says to the Groom, "But the guests can insult your wife."
Father?	when he says, "Those modern writers are always dragging family life in the mud. When it's the best thing we Germans have."
Mother?	when she says to the Groom, "Don't splash your nice waistcoat with the wine. There's a spot on it already."

■ What does this exercise tell you about each of these characters?

■ How can you use these ideas in your portrayal of the roles?

59
56
63
59
57

COMPARING TEXTS

This is an extract from a review of a performance of the play:

Polly Hemingway wasn't only very pretty as the Bride, her performance too was delicious to watch. First she shows us the self-confident young woman bursting with pride for her beautiful self-made home; as the evening wears on and her 'respectability' is somewhat cracked (her husband turns out to be an incompetent craftsman, her sister is an outrageous flirt, and worst of all, her pregnancy is discovered) she becomes more and more bitter, a potential house-dragon, who is dreading the monotonous life that is to start on the morning after her wedding-party ...

The only disappointment was Daniel Geroll's performance as the Bridegroom's Friend. Mr Geroll was obviously just as fed up with his part as was his character with the wedding reception. This was doubly regrettable, as the Bridegroom's Friend is, of course, the key figure ...

Ria Julian, *Plays and Players*, February 1979

◆3I Discussion

- What is Ria Julian's opinion of these two performances in the play? What reasons does this reviewer give for their views, if any?
- How does this view of the characters compare with your own interpretation of the roles in the play?

This is an extract from the screenplay of *Four Weddings and a Funeral* written in 1993 by Richard Curtis.

Scene 23. Exterior. Marquee. Reception. Day.

Throughout the reception, the background action should be full of the business of weddings: waiters and waitresses at work, band tuning up, people chatting and laughing.

CUT TO: **Charles** *winding through people. He spies* **Carrie,** *but she is headed off by a good-looking man – she is clearly much fêted.*

CHARLES Bastard.

He heads for the drinks table to stock up. By the time he turns, she's alone again. He makes it to her.

CHARLES O – hello. Want one of these?

CARRIE Thank you.

CHARLES Ahm …

Just as he's searching for what to say, an acquaintance slips into shot: he's a rather stiff, 38-going-on-60 stockbroker.

JOHN Hello, Charles.

CHARLES Hello, dear John – how are you? … This is …

CARRIE Carrie.

JOHN Delighted, I'm John.

Tiny pause – who's to talk?

CHARLES So, John – how's that gorgeous girlfriend of yours?

JOHN She is no longer my girlfriend.

CHARLES O dear – still, I wouldn't get too gloomy – rumour has it she never stopped bonking old Toby de Lisle, just in case you didn't work out.

JOHN She is now my wife.

CHARLES Excellent. Excellent. Congratulations.

Carrie *takes in totally that this is the most embarrassing moment and leaves them to it, amused.*

◆3m Types of comedy: discussion and writing

1. In what ways is the comedy in this scene similar or different to that of *A Respectable Wedding*? Which do you prefer, and why?

2. Write a scene set at a wedding. Decide on your own characters and create a comic situation which results in someone saying or doing something which is inappropriate but which an audience would find funny.

Answer to task 3h

Maria (Bride); Ina (Bride's Sister); Hans Mildner (Young Man); Jacob (Groom); Emmy (Wife).

Two Marias

Bryony Lavery

BRYONY LAVERY

Bryony Lavery was born in 1947 and grew up in Dewsbury, Yorkshire. She has worked as a director, performer and teacher as well as being the writer of over 20 stage plays. Her early work was with many important theatre groups such as Monstrous Regiment, The Women's Theatre Group and Gay Sweatshop and she has also been involved in writing for children's theatre. Her plays often deal with dark subjects like serial killers (*Frozen* – written in 1997, produced at the National Theatre in 2002), Alzheimer's disease (*A Wedding Story* – first performed at the Birmingham Repertory Theatre in 2000) and cannibalism (*More Light* – written as part of the BT National Theatre Connections project in 1996). Lavery herself says that, "I'm good on grief, death and anger," and the exploration of these themes can be seen in this extract from *Two Marias*, written for Theatre Centre Women's company in 1989.

SUMMARY OF THE PLOT

The inspiration for the play was an extraordinary newspaper story about two Spanish girls, both called Maria, who were involved in a car accident: Maria del Morte was killed and Maria del Amor was badly injured. In the ambulance on the way to the hospital, the handbags of the two girls got mixed up and the two girls were mistaken for each other. The family of Maria del Amor never see the corpse of Maria del Morte and they bury her thinking that she is their own daughter.

Meanwhile, Maria del Amor is recovering in hospital, badly disfigured and covered in bandages. The parents of Maria del Morte are led to believe that their daughter has survived the accident. Gradually both the authorities and Maria del Morte's sister realize the mistake and Maria del Amor is reunited with her rightful family whilst the family of Maria del Morte have to rebury the body of their dead child.

Bryony Lavery retells the story by having the mourning mother of Maria del Morte, Marguerita, turn up in the courtyard of the home of an unrelated girl also named Maria and her mother, Julia. Mother and daughter are arguing because Maria has declared that she is in love with another girl and Julia feels that this lesbian relationship will bring shame on the family. Marguerita shares the pain of her loss with Maria and Julia and this in turn invokes the ghost of her dead daughter. Maria del Morte is a presence in the play and the living Maria experiences the feelings of what it must be like to lose your own mother. Similarly, Julia identifies with the pain that Marguerita is feeling and this brings about a stronger bond between herself and her own daughter, Maria.

THE SCENE IN CONTEXT

This is the point in the play when it becomes apparent that the supposedly living Maria del Morte is in fact Maria del Amor and that a tragic mistake has been made. Marguerita reveals that she knew instinctively that the living Maria was not her own Maria but that she was desperately clinging onto the idea of her being still alive. Having the living Maria taken from her makes her loss seem even more tragic. After Marguerita leaves, a sense of reconciliation is created between Julia and Maria.

Two Marias

By

Bryony Lavery – UK

CAST LIST

MARGUERITA a fifty-year-old woman
MARIA DEL MORTE the ghost figure of Marguerita's dead daughter
JULIA Maria's mother
MARIA a young woman

Setting

A courtyard outside a Spanish house. There are benches, chairs, terracotta pots on three sides. On the fourth side, the house. The ground is dusty. There is fierce light and heat in some of the courtyard, deep cool shade elsewhere.

MARIA DEL MORTE Two families suffer. In Camas, a mother believes her daughter has lost her life. In Huelva, a mother believes her daughter has lost her memory.

MARGUERITA *(to the two **Marias**)* Look … *(She takes a newspaper and begins tearing it.)* There once was a land with no trees.

Maria del Morte smiles in recognition.

MARGUERITA And it was very hot … and the people had no shade. *(She keeps tearing.)* So they went to the wisest old woman of the land and said "Make us a tree". *(She keeps tearing.)* So she did. *(She starts pulling from the centre of the newspaper and out comes a newspaper palm tree.)* She made them a tree. *(She pulls out some more.)* And it grew and grew and grew. *(It grows and grows and grows.)* Until she had made them a very tall tree. And all the people in the land were happy.

Maria del Morte claps, **Maria** *does not.*

MARGUERITA Here … *(She gives the tree to* **Maria**.*)*

MARIA DEL MORTE The mother in Huelva tries to remind her daughter of the past.

MARGUERITA Don't you remember the tree story? Don't you remember the tree? You must remember all the trees I made …

MARIA DEL MORTE She begs …

MARGUERITA When you were a little girl … you were always saying …

MARIA DEL MORTE Make me a tree to sleep under …

MARGUERITA Make me a tree to sleep under …

MARIA DEL MORTE But the new Maria does not remember the tree …

MARIA I remember another tree … *(to* **Julia***)* Do you remember the picnic we had at the Fluvia?

JULIA In your yellow dress …

MARIA That you said I shouldn't wear because I would spoil it …

JULIA It was your newest dress … for a picnic …

MARIA And I cried and cried …

JULIA You shrieked and yelled …

MARIA And finally you said …

JULIA 'God in Heaven … if it's so important, wear the bloody dress … but don't blame me if anything happens to it!!!'

MARIA And I went to the River Fluvia in my new yellow dress.

JULIA And I went to the River Fluvia in a stinking temper!

MARIA And I climbed that tree …

JULIA Overhanging the River Fluvia …

Maria And the branch was slippy and I ...

Julia Fell splash into the River Fluvia ...

Maria And you waded in and fished me out ...

Julia So we both got soaked in the River Fluvia!

Maria And then Mama ...

Julia And then I looked at you ... your yellow dress ... khaki ... with the mud of Fluvia and me ... khaki with the mud of Fluvia ... and I laughed and laughed and laughed ...

Maria Yes. It's the same thing now, Mama.

Julia No.

Maria Yes. Let me put on my yellow dress because I'm happy. Let me climb the trees because I'm well and happy.

Julia And if you fall!!!

Maria Let me fall!!!

Julia Into this stinking disgusting mud which will cover us all ...

Maria Laugh at it! Look at me and laugh ... because I am happy!!!

Julia Listen to me ... just as I waded into the river and dragged you from the mud of Fluvia ... so will I wade in and drag you from this mud you wallow in now!!!

Maria Aaaaagh! *(She flings the paper tree at **Julia**.)*

Maria Del Morte What would you have felt, Mother ... if I had fallen in love with a girl?

Marguerita I would have felt as she felt. No mother wants this pain for her daughter.

Maria Del Morte Or joy either? Enrique Boyer, our therapist, is confused. His patient, Maria, grows physically stronger every day. But what, oh what of her mind? She lives ... in Huelva. *(She draws its position in the dust.)* Her name is Maria del Morte ... But why, oh why, does she insist on calling herself Maria del Amor ...

and giving her address as Camas ... seventy miles away and in a different province? *(She draws its position in the dust.)* Why does a girl from here ... Huelva ... a student of history in Huelva ... know the telephone number of a bar of a beautician's school in Seville? *(draws in Seville ... studies the puzzle)* He is puzzled. How can he explain it? He decides to go back to the start, to the accident ... He searches out the accident report and discovers that it took place at Punta Umbria ... midway between Camas and Huelva ... and discovers that the driver of one car was Maria del Morte, the driver of the other car Maria del Amor who lived in Camas, who now lies buried in the cemetery in Camas. Why has Maria del Morte taken on the details of the dead girl's life? What is your name?

MARIA Mud.

MARIA DEL MORTE Where do you live?

MARIA Here. There. Nowhere.

MARIA DEL MORTE What is your mother's name?

*No answer from **Maria**.*

MARIA DEL MORTE What's your father's name?

*No answer from **Maria**.*

MARIA DEL MORTE Tell me about your accident ...

MARIA Leave me alone ...

MARIA DEL MORTE Perhaps, thinks Boyer, the girl has overheard the name of Maria del Amor, the address of Maria del Amor, in the confusion after the accident ... What do you remember of your accident?

MARIA I was not in this accident!

MARIA DEL MORTE His theory takes hold.

MARIA There's a river that flows ... and ... you're little ... and it seems a long way across to the other bank ... so ... you stay on your own side … the water up to your ankles … and then you go in a bit deeper … to your knees … and the current flows past you … pulling your legs … up to your waist … up to your chest … and all the time … the other bank gets closer … until one day … you're swimming … and you could do it … you could reach the other side … but by then … you can swim … and the current's pulling you the other way … downstream … because that way's longer … rivers are longer than they are wide … and you want to go that way … not across to the other bank.

Maria Del Morte Enrique Boyer, with his incomplete knowledge, believes that her sanity is flowing away …

Maria I'll swim.

Julia Against the current! It's hard swimming against the current.

Maria I'm swimming the way I want …

Julia It's the wrong way!!!

Maria Del Morte Enrique Boyer reluctantly considers the use of electric shock.

Maria Nooooo!!!! *(takes newspaper and reads)* 'Two sisters, aged twelve and nineteen, who were kept captive almost all of their lives by their mother, have been freed. The mother, widow Maria Kolb, 48, feared the girls would catch some disease in the outside world. The elder girl, Eva, had spent only six days at primary school, and her sister, Heidi-Marie, had never been to one. The only time they escaped from their home in Bayreuth, Bavaria, was several years ago when their grandmother took them shopping while their mother was out. Police said Mrs Kolb threatened to kill the girls and herself when they went to free them. They found a loaded revolver under a cushion in her living room. The girls looked dazed when taken from their home.'

Looked dazed, looked dazed, look dazed, Maria Kolb, Eva Kolb, Heidi-Marie Kolb. *(She goes down on her knees and starts writing in the dust.)*

Maria del Morte *stands and looks at what she is writing.*

Maria Del Morte *(reads)* 'To what there is … there is … what there isn't' … to what there is there is what there isn't … Enrique Boyer took the girl's scribbling as a plea for help …

Maria Help me … somebody please help me … please, please, somebody help me …

Maria Del Morte Enrique Boyer decided to try another tack.

*Marguerita takes a small book from her bag, and shows it to **Julia**.*

Marguerita Dictionary. I have lately been looking up the meaning of words …

Maria Del Morte Boyer came from Catalunya … in the far north of Spain …

Marguerita I need to know exactly what the words mean … do you understand?

Maria Del Morte In the opposite corner from Andalucía … where now he worked …

Marguerita Words such as love … such as death … such as mother … do you know?

Maria Del Morte But as it happened … one of the few people he knew in Andalucía was a doctor from Camas …

Marguerita When they said 'She is dead' … I need to know what that means …

Maria Del Morte The doctor was his friend. It was an extraordinary coincidence.

Marguerita Coincidence. *(starts looking up the word)* Two girls … seventeen … in two cars … named Maria … meet in the same terrible moment … *(reads)* 'a chance occurrence of events … remarkable for apparently being connected … '

Maria Del Morte 'It was an extraordinary coincidence' said Boyer … Camas is a very small town … and Spain a very big country!

Marguerita What is an accident? Why my daughter? Why her?

Maria Del Morte Enrique Boyer asks his doctor to come and look at Maria del Morte. Perhaps he will understand why the girl keeps calling 'Amor Amor'. The doctor looks at the girl. He stares. He goes outside. Leans against the wall. 'But this girl is Maria del Amor, Curro Romero Street, Camas,' he says. 'This is Maria del Amor!'

Marguerita starts crying.

Maria Del Morte The doctor from Camas goes back to the little town ... he tells Toni Reina ... the girl's aunt ...

Marguerita Like spies ... traitors ... behind my back ... the doctors plot ...

Maria Del Morte Toni Reina comes to the clinic at Huelva ...

Marguerita I let her go to the clinic because I thought they were mending her ...

Maria Del Morte Toni Reina looks at her niece 'Do you know who I am?' she asks. Maria del Amor nods calmly.

Marguerita How could she know?

Maria Del Morte Toni Reina tells the Mayor of Camas. They start to collect evidence to reclaim the daughter of their town. Frequently, the mayor meets the parents of Maria del Amor on the street ... he cannot sleep for he is weighted down with his secret.

Marguerita No one told me this was happening! Behind my back.

Maria Del Morte Then the mayor tells the parents of Maria del Amor. It is arranged for the father to see Maria del Amor in the Huelva clinic.

Marguerita Still nobody tells us!

Maria Del Morte The father looks at the girl. He is in anguish. He wants to shout ... to take her in his arms ... to hold her safe. Maria del Amor registers no surprise at seeing her father.

She smiles. She puts her finger to her lips and says "Shhh. Otherwise they'll leave me here."

MARGUERITA Shhh. Otherwise they'll leave me here.

MARIA DEL MORTE Maria del Amor's father goes to the police to demand the return of his daughter. What did this family want with his daughter? How could they not know that Maria del Amor was not their child?

MARGUERITA All this time ... I am letting her go to the clinic, believing they are making her well. My husband is called in. He is shown photograph albums of the girl. He tells my son Antonio ... 'It's not your sister ... it's someone else ... I have seen an album full of photographs of the girl' ... It all becomes clear to them ... all the doubts ... the painted toe-nails ... the missing mark on her thigh ... so. So ... my family do not have the courage to tell me the truth ... they say Maria is needed for urgent tests ... and my husband escorts her round the corner ... where her father waits with two police officers. And on August the first ... for the second time ... my daughter is taken away from me forever.

There is silence.

JULIA How could you not know that she was not yours?

No answer.

Marguerita *takes a newspaper and starts to tear it.*

JULIA For seventeen years you held this girl ... you fed her at your breast ... you looked with wonder on her every day ... knowing she was yours ... when she fell down ... you kissed her face and rubbed her knee and saw that she was better ... when she cried ... you hurt ... when she screamed you felt the pain in your heart ... when she fell into danger ... you were gripped at the throat with fear ... How could you not know that she was not your child???

Marguerita *says nothing. She continues tearing her newspaper.*

JULIA And somewhere ... all this time ... was a mother ... just like you ... feeling as you feel ... sitting in a dark room ... lit by one lamp ... staring into the night ... thinking no thought but this ... my daughter is dead ... I cannot understand it ... my daughter is dead! How could you do it? *(She goes to **Maria**.)* Maria ... whatever you are ... whatever I am ... I know one thing ... you are my daughter ... and I love you more than life. Let us go into the house and I will block your door shut with a chair so that ghosts cannot come and take you.

MARIA Mama. No. What you fear for me can't be held by a chair against a door. A thousand chairs against a thousand doors will not keep it out. Something has come and taken me. The ghosts are here.

MARIA DEL MORTE My body was dug up and brought back from Camas to Huelva. I was returned to my family. My parents were too upset to identify me. They asked my brother, Antonio, to look at me ... see that it was me. After two months in the coffin ... my looks had gone. I had decomposed badly. My skin had blackened. The smell was nauseous. But Antonio could recognise me instantly. "It was horrible," he says. "When I see a photograph of my sister now, or when I talk about her, the image of her all black inside the coffin comes back to me. I can't get rid of it." He does not sleep now ... for I can come through a thousand doors. *(She smiles.)* The one advantage of being dead. I may visit where I please ... whenever I please ...

(sings)

A thousand chairs
Against a thousand doors
A thousand doors
In a thousand walls
Will not keep me away
I will come to you
A thousand keys
Turned in a thousand locks
A thousand links
In a thousand chains
Will not keep me away
I will come to you ...

Staging the extract

SET AND PROPS

The period of the play is the late 1980s but it can be easily updated to the present day. There are several references to Spanish towns and people with Spanish sounding names and this locates the play quite specifically. The setting can be quite simple but the props and atmosphere need to suggest the heat and characteristics of Spain.

The play was originally performed in school halls with the audience on four sides of a Spanish courtyard. The diagram below shows how the play would work in an "in-the-round" setting.

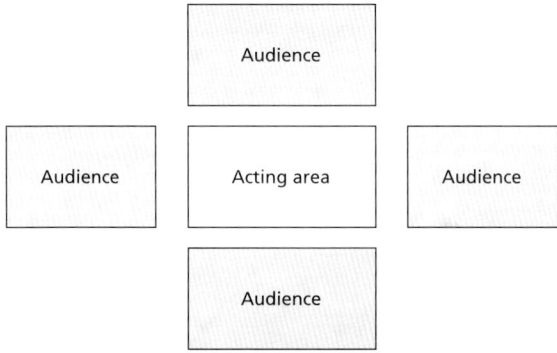

◆4a Making a ground plan

Organization: Work in small groups.

Task:

- Read the extract from the point of view of making decisions about the positioning of entrances, exits, furniture and items of set dressing.
- Decide on the size of the acting area and copy out the set diagram to a scale of 1:25.

- Mark on the diagram the exit and entrance into the house, and the exit and entrance from the courtyard out to the street. The remaining two exits between the audience can be used as positions for furniture and set dressing.
- Mark on the diagram the position of benches and chairs.

◆4b Design research

Carry out the following research tasks and use your findings to put together a visual display that will inform the visual appearance of the setting and the props.

- Find out where the following places are in Spain: Camas, Huelva, Fluvia, Seville, Punta Umbria, Catalunya, Andalucía.
- Collect some images of houses from this part of Spain, especially any with courtyards. Identify the kind of outdoor furniture, pots and plants that can be seen in this part of the world.
- The floor of the courtyard is dusty. How could you create this effect? What colour and texture would it be?
- Marguerita makes a "growing" palm tree by tearing it out of newspaper. Investigate how this is done and make a sample prop from newspaper.

 ## COSTUME AND MAKE-UP

The costumes and make-up should show the difference in the age of the characters. Marguerita is 50, Maria and Maria del Morte are both 17 and Julia is in her mid to late 30s. With the older characters it is possible to use more typically Spanish clothing to provide a sense of place (see photo on page 98). Maria can be dressed in the fashion worn by any typical 17-year-old. The climate is hot, so she is likely to be wearing something light and colourful. Make-up can be used to create the effects of age and living in a sunny climate. Maria del Morte is an interesting design challenge both in terms of make-up and costume because she is the spirit of someone who is dead.

◆4c Discussion: Ghost stories

Organization: Work in a group of four or five. You will need a flip chart and some pens.

Task: Think about a film or a play that you have seen which features a ghost or ghosts. Ask for a volunteer from the group to act as a sketch artist. Each person in turn describes what the ghost looked like in their selected play or film. The sketch artist tries to draw it from the description and the person describing can ask them to alter bits as they go along. You will end up with four or five ghost pictures to look at. From these sketches, put together a picture of the ghost in the play. How might you create the visual effects using make-up and costume?

LIGHTING

The stage direction for the play says, "There is fierce light and heat in some of the courtyard, deep cool shade elsewhere." There are no lighting changes as such in the scene, although the play ends at suppertime.

84

◆4d Lighting design decisions

Organization: You will need to use a copy of the ground plan produced for the set design in task 4a. On it should be marked where the house and the exit from the courtyard are.

Task: Consider these questions:

- What provides shade from the sun?
- How can you create shade on stage?
- Which direction is the sun going to be shining from on stage?
- Which areas are going to be brightly lit and which areas dimly lit?
- Are any colours being used?

Extension: Using the lanterns and control system available, experiment with the lighting to create the atmosphere for the courtyard in the play.

Exploring the extract

HISTORICAL AND CULTURAL CONTEXT

This is a contemporary play, based on a car accident that happened on 2 June 1987, that deals with the universal theme of the loss of a daughter by her mother. Despite all the advances of medical science, it takes several months for the doctors to realize that the Maria who is still alive is in fact the one that they thought was dead. The play is set in Spain, a Catholic country, and this may have some effect on the way the characters think and feel.

♦4e Research and writing

1. **Research**
   Investigate the way in which funerals are carried out in Spain. What sorts of rites and rituals take place? What does a Spanish graveyard look like? Draw a picture of Maria del Amor's monument or tombstone.

2. **Writing**
   Imagine that you are a newspaper journalist covering the story of the funeral of Maria del Amor and write a 150–200-word article to send into your editor describing the funeral, the events that led up to it and the behaviour of the mourners.

SUBJECT MATTER

Bryony Lavery says that, "it is a play for those scared of losing their loved ones to some unimaginable tragedy." The subject matter of the play is grief and how Marguerita is coming to terms with it. Parents expect their children to outlive them and it is always deeply tragic when a son or daughter dies or is killed at a young age, having experienced less of life that their father and mother.

◆4f Still images

Organization: Working in groups of three or four, create a series of images that show the following situations:

A. a mother and/or father with their son or daughter at a moment in their lives when they are proud of some achievement. (For example, the son or daughter has won a prize at school or they have passed all their exams.)

B. a mother and/or father receiving the news from a doctor, nurse or policeman that their son or daughter is dead

C. a mother and/or father at the funeral of their child.

Follow up: Show each of the still images in turn to the rest of your class. Ask the class to identify how the different situations are shown through body language and positioning.

Extension: Record each of your still images using a digital camera and capture them on a computer. Add thought bubbles and write in the thoughts for the characters in each of the still images. Use presentation software to project your work onto a screen so that the rest of the class can discuss it.

GENRE

The genre of the play is difficult to categorize because Bryony Lavery has a unique way of writing that combines naturalism, poetry, song, symbolism and yet is also a kind of ghost story. At the end of the play Julia asks, "Did that … just then …" and Maria replies, "No! Don't say … Pretend we read it in the newspapers." This suggests that Julia and Maria belong to the real world and that Marguerita and Maria del Morte have been part of a visionary or imaginary world.

*A Spanish woman dressed in clothing
typical for widows of her generation*

◆4g Narration and writing

Scenario: Imagine that you are Maria some 20 years later looking back at the strange day that an old woman and the ghost of her dead daughter appeared in the courtyard of your house. You are going to retell the story in the role of a narrator.

Task: Write your own version of the events of the day and decide which parts of the story you are going to narrate and which parts you are going to act out by using selected parts of the script.

Extension: Rehearse your version of the play and act it out. Take part in an after-show discussion to gauge the audience's response to your version of the story.

Exploring characters

Each of the characters in the play is trying to come to terms with an important event in their lives.

◆4h Point of view exercise

Organization: Work in four groups of three or four people. Group A is the "Julia" group; Group B is the "Marguerita" group; Group C is the "Maria" group; Group D is the "Maria del Morte" group. Each group has a copy of the speech below spoken by their character.

Task 1: One person in the group takes on the role of their named character and acts out the speech several times. The rest of the group makes notes as they listen and watch. Write down any thoughts you have about the character's feelings, thoughts or attitudes and any questions you want to ask them.

Task 2: The note-takers in each group now have an opportunity to interview their character and to build up a broader picture of their personality.

Task 3: Each group nominates a spokesperson. Each spokesperson in turn is going to report back their findings to the whole class so that everyone gets to find out the points of view of each of the four characters.

Group A Julia You cannot do this!! You cannot!! You are my daughter and you will bring shame on me! … Love? … Love? … She is a girl! You can't … You're mad! … You're sick! … You need locking up! … I wish you'd never been born!!! What kind of life is that??? No husband, no children, no family … everyone despising you? You'll have no life! I'll take you to the priest … I'll take you to the doctor … what's your father going to … And what do you think you're doing to me? You're making me crazy!!! Maria … Please!!!

Group B Marguerita This happened. Imagine it. It is a hot summer night. My daughter Maria decided to go for a swim. She said goodbye. Imagine too, that your daughter Maria also decided to go for a swim. She says goodbye. It is eight-thirty, 2 June 1987 and your Maria's car rounds the curve that leads through the pine woods to the long beach at Punta Umbria. Suddenly, a car in the opposite lane swerves off the asphalt and throws up a shower of gravel which shatters the windscreen of the Renault behind. Blinded, the driver of the Renault veers into the oncoming lane and, at 40 miles an hour, slams into the car carrying your daughter. She breaks her ankle frantically trying to brake ... then crushes her chest on the steering wheel as the force of the crash heaves her, face first, through the windscreen.

Group C Maria Here's what I'm going to do tonight. After supper ... I'm going to put on my ... blue dress... yes... and I'll go to Felipe's because ... because they play good music ... and everybody'll be there ... and Paula ... she'll be there ... and we'll all have a good time ... we'll dance with the boys ... Pepe ... and Juan-Carlos ... and Michelito ... and then ... we'll get in Paula's car ... just Paula and me ... and we'll drive with the windows open so we can smell the pine ... through the woods ... by the twisty road ... down to the beach for a swim. And when we're in the water ... I might, I just might get hold of Paula ... and kiss her dead on the lips! Yes!

Group D	Maria del Morte	I go into the curve of a long, long bend ... the gravel under the wheels is loose ... the car bucks ... skids ... there's a car coming towards me ... there's a car coming right at me. The wheel won't turn ... there's a girl coming at me through the windscreen ... the windscreen's gone blank ... it's snow, it's ice, it's burning my face, it's cutting my face, it's in my eyes, into my head, it's slicing my brain into pieces of gravel, what is happening? Where am I? Who am I? I am in pieces all over the road!! ... I was a dreadful sight! So, while the new Maria del Morte lay ill in hospital I was buried, as Maria del Amor, in a strange cemetery, seventy miles from my home ... mourned by a family I had never met.

MARIA DEL MORTE

Maria del Morte says to Maria: "I was tall and slender with light brown hair. She, like you, had a pug nose, slightly plumper ... with short chestnut hair ... and a brace on her teeth. Nobody could have mistaken us for each other. But that is what happened." This says something about Maria del Morte's physical appearance when she was alive but the challenge for an actor is how to play a character that is a living corpse. This character functions in the play as a way of retelling the events of the past, but also as a way of enabling Marguerite to come to terms with her loss. Later in the play, just before Maria del Morte leaves, she says, "The one advantage of a dead daughter is that she can visit where she pleases ... when she pleases ... I will come through a thousand doors to you to the end of your life. And then, perhaps, you will come to me."

♦4i **Thought tunnel**

The purpose of this exercise is to put the appropriate thoughts into the head of the person playing the role of Maria del Morte so that they can enter the scene and convey the mood of the character. *cont...*

> **Maria del Morte**
>
> The group creates two straight lines of people standing and facing each other with a gap (or "tunnel") of about one metre between them. A person in the role of Maria del Morte walks through the tunnel and hears thoughts about her character or situation from the people to either side. Each person making up the tunnel must be prepared to provide a thought. For example: "Why are you still haunting your mother?"; "I wish I were still alive". When "Maria del Morte" has walked through the tunnel, she speaks her thoughts for everyone to hear. Everyone can have an opportunity at walking through the tunnel and new thoughts and ideas can be added at any time.

MARGUERITA

Marguerita opens the play with the lines, "This house is full of pain./ Feel it in my heart./ Oh … the ache./ It answers mine" which set the tone of her character for the play. She has suffered by trying to believe that a girl called Maria del Amor was truly her own daughter who has survived the car accident and then been confronted with the tragic news that the body that has been buried is that of her own daughter. During the play, she relives the events of the past by playing them out through the senses of a younger mother, Julia and her daughter, Maria. Her pain evokes the spirit of her dead daughter who appears in the play to help her deal with her grief.

◆4j Role-play

Organization: Work in pairs, one person role-playing Marguerita and the other her daughter, Maria.

Situation 1: Marguerita is looking through a photograph album and remembering her daughter as a child. The ghost of Maria appears and speaks to her.

Opening line: **MARIA:** "Mother, you know that the girl in the other room is not me …"

Situation 2: The body of Maria has just been reburied in Huelva and Marguerita is visiting the grave. The ghost of Maria appears.

Opening line: **MARIA:** "Mother, you can let go now, I am gone …"

MARIA

During the play, Maria remembers moments of her childhood with her mother and also takes on the persona of the other two Marias in the story. What effect does meeting Marguerita and Maria del Morte have on Maria? How has it altered her relationship with her own mother?

◆4k Crossing the circle

The group stands in a circle and one person is chosen to start the exercise. The chosen person is going to walk towards someone on the other side of the circle and speak to them as if she or he is Maria in the play. For example, they could say, "You are very lucky not to have been killed in that accident." The person spoken to replies in the role of Maria. For example, "But it was Marguerita's daughter in the accident, not me." The person who crossed the circle stands next to the person who "became" Maria. The person who replied as Maria now has a turn at spotting someone on the other side of the circle and asking them a question, which they reply to in the role of Maria. What impression do you have of Maria as a character at the end of this exercise?

JULIA

Julia is a mother who has reached a point in her life where she knows she has to let go of her daughter and allow her to live her own life. During the play she goes through the transition of seeing Maria as a child to seeing her as a young adult. Julia's love for her daughter is unconditional, "you are my daughter … and I love you more than life," but she cannot protect Maria from feeling what she feels for another woman and she must start to come to terms with this. The context of the play shows Julia that her situation with her daughter pales into insignificance compared to that of Marguerita and her daughter.

92

♦4| Writing and role-play

Situation: It is six months since Marguerita visited your house and you have managed to find out where she lives. Maria has left home to live with her girlfriend, Paula.

Task 1: Write a letter to Marguerita thanking her for the blessing she put on your house and the change it has made to your life.

Task 2: Work in pairs. Person A is Julia writing a letter. Person B is Marguerita reading the letter she has received. Create a scene that shows Julia and Marguerita in two different parts of the stage. Use lights to spot the two areas if they are available. Decide which parts of the letter the audience hears and sees Julia writing, and which parts Marguerita is seen and heard reading.

How does this exercise help you understand what Julia experiences in the play?

COMPARING TEXTS

This is an extract from *Blood Wedding* written in 1933 by the Spanish playwright Federico Garcia Lorca. This scene deals with a mother coming to terms with her son's desire to get married. The mother believes that the bride comes from a family of murderers because her husband and her other son have been killed by members of the girl's family.

BRIDEGROOM What about me, mother?

MOTHER You? What?

BRIDEGROOM Do I need to tell you again?

MOTHER *(serious)* Ah!

BRIDEGROOM Do you think it's a bad idea?

MOTHER No.

BRIDEGROOM Well then?

MOTHER I'm not sure. It's so sudden like this. It's taken me by surprise. I know that the girl's good. She is, isn't she? Well-behaved. Hard-working. She makes her bread and she sews her skirts. But even so, when I mention her name, it's as if they were pounding my head with a stone.

BRIDEGROOM Don't be silly.

MOTHER It's more than silly. I'll be left alone. Only you are left to me now and I'm sorry to see you going.

BRIDEGROOM But you'll come with us.

MOTHER No. I can't leave your father and your brother here. I have to go to them every morning, and if I leave, one of the Felixes could die, one of the family of murderers, and they'd bury him next to mine. I won't stand for that. Never that! Because I'll dig them up with my nails and all on my own I'll smash them to bits against the wall.

BRIDEGROOM (*strongly*) Back to that again!

Translated by Gwynne Edwards

♦4m Discussion

Both the mother in *Blood Wedding* and Julia in *Two Marias* have strong reservations about the people that their respective son and daughter have fallen in love with.

■ Why do parents feel that they have a right to question their children about the kind of people they can or cannot go out with?

■ What is your own parents' attitude to your friends?

■ Are sons and daughters treated any differently?

Exploring and comparing the four extracts

RITES AND RITUALS

The plays in this collection involve the rites and rituals surrounding love and death. In each of the plays, there is something unusual about the rite or ritual that takes place. In *The Shaughraun*, the rite of an Irish wake is turned on its head because the ritual of a funeral is about to take place of someone who is, in fact, alive. Oscar Wilde turns the ritual of a marriage proposal into a ridiculous situation because Lady Bracknell does not want her daughter marrying someone who was born in a handbag. Whilst the wedding in Brecht's play might be respectable, the fact that the furniture that the bridegroom has built is beginning to collapse suggests otherwise. It is customary when someone dies for some kind of funeral rite to take place, but because a mistake is made in identifying the *Two Marias*, the funeral of Marguerita del Morte takes place twice.

TWO FUNERALS

♦5a Discussion

⟨⟨ ⟩⟩

1. How is the subject of death treated in *The Shaughraun* and in *Two Marias*?

2. What would Maria's funeral have been like compared to that of Conn's?

◆5b Writing

Situation 1: Imagine that you are a journalist on a local newspaper.

Task 1: Write a 100–150 word article with an appropriate headline, reporting the funerals of Conn (*The Shaughraun*) and Maria (the first funeral of Maria del Amor) in a local newspaper.

Situation 2: The following week the news breaks that Conn is, in fact, alive and is to be married to Moya Dolan.

Task 2: Write a follow-up article correcting your previous report and explaining how a funeral has now become a wedding.

Situation 3: Two months later, you receive an anonymous phone call telling you that a body of a girl in Camas is being dug up and moved 70 miles away to Huelva. The funeral you reported on before should have been for Maria del Morte.

Task 3: Write an exclusive story for your paper on the strange events surrounding two funerals for the same Maria.

◆5c Improvization

Organization: Work in a group of between five and nine. Devise a drama that has a funeral as its starting point. One person takes on the role of the Vicar and each of the other people in the group is somehow related to the person who has just died. For example, Mother, Brother, Lover, Friend, Boss.

Situation: The drama begins with the funeral service. Devise a series of flashback scenes that show the dead person's relationship with the people at his or her funeral. Each person has a reason for being happy or sad that the person is dead. The drama ends with the mourners in a "freeze-frame" as the ghost of the dead person appears and says what they think of each of the people at the funeral. You should try and maintain the tension throughout the drama by giving clues as to the person's cause of death but not revealing it until the end. You will need to decide how and why the person died.

cont...

> *Opening line:* **VICAR:** "Forasmuch as it hath pleased Almighty God of his great mercy to take unto himself the soul of our dear [*brother/sister*] here departed, we therefore commit [*his/her*] body to the ground; earth to earth, ashes to ashes, dust to dust; in sure and certain hope of the resurrection to eternal life through our Lord Jesus Christ; who shall change the body of our low estate that it may be like unto his glorious body, according to the mighty working, whereby he is able to subdue all things to himself."

◆5d Research

- Different cultures have their own rites and rituals for burying the dead. The Vicar's speech quoted above is one used at a Christian burial. Find out the attitudes of other cultures to the dead and how funerals or equivalent rites for the dead are carried out.

- Use your research to create the improvisation in 5c in a different cultural setting.

TWO WEDDINGS

The scene from *The Importance of Being Earnest* illustrates the ritual of a marriage proposal, whilst the scene from *A Respectable Wedding* shows the events after the wedding ceremony. In neither play do we see the actual wedding itself.

◆5e Still image

Organization: Work in two groups of at least ten people. Group A will depict the wedding ceremony that takes place between Gwendolen and Ernest, and Group B will depict the wedding ceremony that takes place between Maria (The Bride) and Jacob (The Groom).

Task: An extract from the Church of England marriage ceremony is given below. Each group is going to act out four still images to accompany this moment in the marriage service. You will need to work out who the guests at the wedding ceremony are and where they are positioned. Show each character's attitude towards the bride and the groom through your facial expressions and body language.

■ Using a digital camera, photograph the still images from each group. In what ways are the two weddings similar or different? How do different people react to the events in the still image? What is going on between the guests in each still image? Which wedding would you rather be a guest at?

VICAR Wilt thou have this woman to thy wedded wife, to live together after God's ordinance in the holy estate of Matrimony? Wilt thou love her, comfort her, honour, and keep her, in sickness and in health; and, forsaking all other, keep thee only unto her, so long as ye both shall live?

MAN I will

VICAR Wilt thou have this man to thy wedded husband, to live together after God's ordinance in the holy estate of Matrimony?

Wilt thou obey him, and serve him, love, honour, and keep him, in sickness and in health; and, forsaking all other, keep thee only unto him, so long as ye both shall live?

WOMAN I will

From the *Church of England Common Prayer Book,* 1662

◆5f Starting points for drama

The following quotations about marriage can be used in a number of ways to start developing your own script for a play. You could use them in any of the following ways:

■ as an opening line spoken by one of your characters

■ as a concluding line for your play

■ as an indication of character from which you can develop further ideas

■ as an idea for a situation in your play.

cont...

A. "I do not think you ever know you are happily married until you have been unhappily married, first." (Angela Carter)

B. "When you see what some girls marry, you realize how they must hate to work for a living." (Helen Rowland)

C. "It should be a very happy marriage – they are both so much in love with *him*." (Irene Thomas)

D. "It is true that I never should have married, but I didn't want to live without a man. Brought up to respect the conventions, love had to end in marriage. I'm afraid it did." (Bette Davis)

Quoted in *Wicked* edited by Fidelis Morgan
(1995, Virago Press, ISBN 1 86049 166 9).